ENDORSEMENTS

"Courage. Grace. Connection. These will get you through. Read all about it right here. Woman courage. Woman power. Female Grace. Female flow. Heart-to-heart connection. Fierce, not feminine at all. This book is a treasure to be savored. A strong thread in the reweaving of the healing cloak of the Ancients."
~ **Susun S. Weed**, Author of *Wise Woman Herbal Series*, Founder of Wise Woman School

"If there were ever a time for Unleashing the Courageous Feminine, it would be now. Ancient matriarchal wisdom resonates in these contemporary women's stories of resilience, rage, and self-liberation. This anthology is an antidote to the silencing and amnesia inflicted by patriarchy, awakening innate wisdom and self-sovereignty."
~ **Vicki Noble**, Co-Creator of *Motherpeace*, Author of *Shakti Woman: Feeling Our Fire, Healing Our World*.

"This rich, inspiring anthology shares stories of thirteen women who healed from the worst ills of patriarchal society ~ erasure of self, incest, rape, and other traumas. Courageously and poignantly, they offer lived experiences of grief, forgiveness, compassion, and rebirth, modeling ways for readers to heal ourselves."
~ **Miriam Robbins Dexter, PhD**, Author of *Whence the Goddesses: A Source Book*

"The female energies rising in women today are key to both personal awakening and the evolution of humanity. These stories will inspire you to walk your soul's unique path of individual and global awakening with greater confidence and courage. They will help you experience your life as a living gift of the Divine Feminine, leading us to the new and harmonious world we all desire."

~ **Marguerite Rigoglioso, PhD**, Author of *The Secret Life of Mother Mary*, Director of Seven Sisters Mystery School.

"...a gift of wild and tender wisdom that unites us all…. These courageous stories, long buried in the body-psyche, emerge as revelations of strength and transformation... A reminder and encouragement on the path, they unleash the courage and wisdom that connect us to ourselves and to humanity."

~ **Camille Maurine**, Author of *Meditation Secrets for Women*

"Unleashing the Divine Feminine is a radiant tapestry of resilience, love, and transformation. Through 13 powerful stories, these women illuminate the path from adversity to awakening, revealing how the Divine Feminine guides us toward healing and wholeness. This book is both an offering and an invocation—an invitation to remember that even in our deepest struggles, grace and strength are always within reach."

~ **Lorie Eve Dechar**, Author of *The Alchemy of Inner Work*

UNLEASHING THE COURAGEOUS FEMININE

13 Stories of Strength, Grace and Awakening Through Adversity

Compiled by Laura Joan Cornell, PhD
Foreword by Camille Maurine

©2025 Laura Joan Cornell – All Rights Reserved
First Printing March 2025
Unleashing the Courageous Feminine –
13 Stories of Strength, Grace and Awakening Through Adversity

All rights reserved. Printed in the United States of America. Ananda Press and Divine Feminine Yoga support the right to free expression and the value of copyright. The purpose of copyright is to encourage writers and artists to produce the creative works that enrich our culture. The scanning, uploading, and distribution of this book without permission is theft of the authors' intellectual properties. If you would like permission to use material from the book (other than for review purposes) please contact: Support@LauraJoanCornell.com
Thank you for your support of the authors' rights.

eBook ISBN: 978-1-7333923-4-1
Paperback ISBN: 978-1-7333923-5-8
Hardcover ISBN: 978-1-7333923-6-5
Ingram Spark ISBN: 978-1-7333923-7-2

Library of Congress Control Number: 2025903818

Copy Editor: Hyla Hitchcox
Cover Artwork: Aimee Tomczak
Cover Design: Sharokin BetGevargiz
Layout Design: Marigold2K
Publisher: Ananda Press

www.divinefeminineyoga.com

Also by the Author

Moon Salutations:
Women's Journey Through Yoga to Healing, Power, and Peace

Awakening the Divine Feminine:
18 Stories of Healing, Inspiration, and Empowerment

Forthcoming:

Unbreakable Spirit:
13 Stories of Feminine Resilience, Blessings, and Renewal

Moon Whispers:
A Guided Journal and Coloring Book for Women

Table of Contents

Dedication ix
Foreword by Camille Maurine xi
Introduction xiii

The Courage of Embodiment: Finding Strength After Amputation

1. A Moment of Tragedy, A Lifetime of Joy
   Shari Dobrin Caradonna 1
2. Unstoppable Elfie: A Journey of Choice and Resilience
   Elfie Knecht 13

Grace From Mother's Line

3. Rosaries of Resilience: From Genocide to Ritual
   Sharokin BetGevargiz 27
4. Intergenerational Gifts Guide the Way
   Sandi Goodwin 43

The Courage to Follow the Inner Voice

5. She Has Risen: Flight of the Phoenix
   Criselda Brooks 55
6. A Walk in the Field of Courage
   Jennifer Andrews 67

The Sacred Feminine and the Power of Compassion

7. Courage, Compassion and Love: My Journey with Mary Magdalene
   Melanie Ann Baron 79
8. How I Met God the Mother
   Shuna Morelli 93

The Courage to Heal; The Strength to Love

9. Ashes Forgiven: The Long Shadow of Sibling Rape
   Angie Merritt 105
10. What Does Love Look Like Here?
    Liz Turnbull 119

The Fierce Grace of the Divine Feminine

11. Medea, The Mother and Me
    Vajra Ma 135
12. The Cauldron, A Bat and Burning down the House
    Diana Will 151

Epilogue

How I Healed from Incest to Awaken to the Divine Feminine Within
Laura Joan Cornell 165

Acknowledgements 177
About the Cover Artist 179
About Divine Feminine Yoga and Ananda Press 181

DEDICATION

To courageous women everywhere.
Thank you for all the ways you light up this planet!

Foreword

Ah, deep breath... we are entering the realm of the heart, a journey of transformation....

Heartache and healing, courage and compassion....

In reading each woman's courageous story, we are taken into her very personal world ~ her life circumstances, challenges, sorrows and joys. These stories may have been held secret for decades, buried deep in the body-psyche waiting for the moment, the context and support, to be remembered and expressed.

Laura Cornell, in creating this book, has provided a fertile context for such excavation and empowerment. Reading each woman's personal experience is an invitation to claim our own ever-deepening awareness. Each story, and the powerful collective context, spark that innate creative intelligence.

Creativity is magic. We create a context for revelation ~ first and foremost, within our own body-psyche. Then we shape the expression in an artful way. Through journaling, writing, telling the story, we discover and excavate buried truths and transform them into inspiration, not only for ourselves, but ultimately on behalf of the entire body of humanity.

Consider this book a reminder and encouragement on the path. On a personal note, I am grateful to read each of these brilliant offerings, including those by Jenn, Vajra Ma, and Laura herself ~

full disclosure, dear friends all. Even now, I glimpse new depths of their brave soul journeys.

My own experience includes creating two full-length solo performances, the first about my mother's tragic life and death, called *Tiger, Tiger*. Becoming my mother in dance and spoken word offered profound insights and strength, as well as copious tears. No sooner did I finish sharing that work then my father died, and his story urged itself into the second piece, *Losing It*, about the stormy father-daughter relationship. These expressions liberated painful memories, transforming them into astonishing freedom and gratitude. And yes, into love ~ a great boon for my now 40+ years of intimacy with my husband, Lorin.

Yes, a prayer of gratitude for the men, perhaps you who read these words. No doubt, as women continue to claim our innate emotional and spiritual intelligence, it benefits the entire energy body of our shared humanity. Yes, women *and* men ~ our family, colleagues, lovers, and friends. Transformation, your time is now.

That is why I celebrate the revelations of courage and strength from each woman in this volume. As you read each potent story, you may find yourself remembering your own. *Unleashing the Courageous Feminine* is a gift of wild and tender wisdom that unites us all.

With you in wonder,
—Camille Maurine

Introduction

We live in a world painfully divided. A recent election in the United States has left deep fissures in our social fabric while similar turmoil is felt in other countries. This political polarization threatens to distract us from the deeper layer of our shared humanity. Amidst today's political turmoil, a powerful force dwells within us, longing to be unleashed: the courageous feminine.

As I began working with the authors of this book, I was struck by the sheer tenacity and strength that resonated within the group. These are women who have faced profound challenges: the loss of a leg, the death of a son, the shattering of a marriage, the insidious erosion of self in an abusive relationship. They have stared despair in the face, contemplated the unthinkable, and ultimately chosen life ~ a life of growth, authenticity, and following the divine voice. They have said "No" to abusive partners, to soul-crushing careers, and to the silent whispers that sought to diminish their worth. They have said "Yes" to their deepest calling.

Even more, woven into this book are stories of profound connection with the Divine Feminine. Within these pages, you will encounter women who have met this divine strength in myriad forms. Some have encountered her on stage, embodying the raw power of Medea. Others felt her presence in the quiet sanctuary of a temple dedicated to Mary Magdalene. Still others discovered her within the depths of their own hearts, in moments of quiet contemplation. She appears as a bat, a cauldron, a flower, a whisper of intuition, or the unwavering strength to utter a simple, yet profound, "No."

These women have found peace amidst the chaos. They have discovered career fulfillment, inner strength, and a deep sense of purpose through their connection to the Divine Feminine. They reflect on the progress women have made over the past 60 years ~ from gaining financial independence to claiming their rightful place in the world of sports ~ while also recognizing the battles that still lie ahead.

Unleashing the Courageous Feminine transcends political divides. It offers a message of hope and healing for all, regardless of political affiliation. It explores themes of courage, strength, grace, and awakening through adversity. It delves into the power of the Divine Feminine to heal, to guide, and to empower ~ qualities desperately needed in our fractured world. You will read stories of:

- **Courage:** The unwavering resolve to stand up to abuse, to reclaim one's voice, and to forge a new path.
- **Strength:** The inner resilience that allows women to navigate loss, trauma, and the most basic challenges of life.
- **Grace:** The ability to move through difficult experiences with dignity, compassion, and an open heart.
- **Awakening through Adversity:** The transformative power of hardship, turning pain into a catalyst for growth and self-discovery.
- **The Divine Feminine:** The profound connection to the sacred feminine principle, a source of wisdom, strength, and unwavering love.

You will meet women who journeyed through the fires of menopause while caring for aging parents, women who reclaimed their ancestral strength after generations of trauma, and women who discovered the transformative power of ritual. You will also encounter stories of profound healing, like that of a woman who, after enduring the trauma of sibling rape, found the strength to care for her brother in his old age. You will encounter astrologers, herbalists, crystal healers, life coaches, yoga and meditation teachers, tour guides, physical therapy assistants, authors, and playwrights ~ women who are sharing their unique gifts with the world.

This book is an invitation ~ an invitation to connect with your own inner strength, to embrace the wisdom of your body, to open your heart to the transformative power of love, and to listen to the whispers of your soul. It is a call to awaken the Divine Feminine within each of us, to reclaim our power, and to create a world where compassion and empathy prevail. It is a call that transcends the noise of our current political climate, reminding us of our shared humanity and our capacity for healing. We are waiting for you. The world is waiting for you. Now is the time to unleash the courageous feminine within.

Chapter 1

A MOMENT OF TRAGEDY, A LIFETIME OF JOY

Shari Dobrin Caradonna, PTA

I have a sign in my room that I look at every morning when I open my eyes. It says, "*You never know how strong you are, until being strong is the only choice you have.*"

It was August 19, 2005, a day my mom and former husband would refer to as the worst day ever. I, on the other hand, often refer to that day as my second birthday, a renewal of my life. It's all about perspective.

I was heading into Manhattan on this bright and sunny day with my beautiful 19-year-old daughter Marissa. We took the train into the city and arrived around 8:30 a.m. We were heading to the Chinese Consulate first, to pick up Marissa's visa, as my girl was leaving in a few weeks to begin an exciting journey. She had chosen to spend a semester abroad in China.

After picking up her visa, we would enjoy some girl time, shopping and then going to meet a friend of mine who worked in the city for lunch. I had planned the perfect day. However, Divine Source, G-D, the powers that be, whatever you may choose to call it, had a plan of its own. I was about to embark on a journey of my own, one that I could never imagine.

As we briskly walked along 11th avenue, we were crossing 38th street right in front of the Jacob Javits Convention Center. Marissa had been walking at a slightly faster pace than I was and was already across the street and up on the curb. I was just a few steps behind her and as I approached the curb...

And I take a deep breath here before continuing to write....

The next few moments were a cross between shock, pain, and disorientation. I suddenly found myself UNDERNEATH a huge private bus. I stared at the front wheel, only to gaze back and see the rear wheel, and looked straight ahead to see coin sized chunks of flesh from my left leg splattered on the ground, my sandal torn in two and my cute white purse strewn far from my reach. OH MY G-D, I was hit by a bus!

Thankfully I don't remember the exact moment of impact, but I surely remember every moment after. "Where is my daughter? Is she okay?" That was my first and only concern. I later found out that the impact had thrown her to the ground, but gratefully she was (physically) okay. As I lay there, I started to take in a little bit of what had just happened and I began to feel the pain. I gently reached down my left leg with my left hand and felt only bone. "OH CRAP!" I thought, "This cannot be good." In a flash of a second, my life became surreal.

Somehow my amazing daughter managed to get back up, saw me lying there underneath the bus, and had the wherewithal to call 911. I simply cannot imagine what on earth could have been going through her head. The fear and disbelief must have shaken her to her core, but there she was, holding it all together for the both of us and making that call.

Luckily for me there was a fire station diagonally across the street and they got to me within a matter of minutes. As they assessed the situation and were figuring out how they were going to get me out, I began to tell them that they needed to stabilize my left leg before they attempted to move me from underneath the bus.

The fireman just looked at me in sheer amazement and asked how I was coherent enough to be giving them guidance and direction. I had no idea, but I knew my baby girl was with me and I was not about to go into shock and disappear on her now. Maybe it was adrenaline, I don't really know, nor do I care. I just needed to be there for her in whatever capacity I could. That's all that mattered to me at that moment. I still didn't even know if she was okay.

They stabilized my leg, pulled me out and got me into the ambulance as quickly as possible. Marissa was seated behind me. As she climbed in, I breathed a huge sigh of relief finally knowing she was indeed okay. She was holding my hand and repeating "Mommy I love you. Mommy you're going to be fine, Mommy let's do our yoga breathing," over and over and over. I was trying to breathe and concentrate on remaining calm and at one point her words seemed to be a distraction and I suddenly said, "Shhh." To which she replied, "Are you shushing me?" It was such an intense moment for both of us. It wasn't funny at that time, but when we talk about it now, it still cracks us up.

We finally got to the hospital, and I was taken into the emergency room with such an urgency that I began wondering just how serious my injury really was. Marissa was taken to a small private room where they had a social worker sit with her until my former husband and my son arrived. She later told me that she casually looked down at her leg and realized there was a chunk of my leg on her leg, and it was stuck there. I cannot imagine what that was like for her. These are the moments that I reflect on every anniversary of this "incident" (I no longer believe in accidents), and it brings tears to my eyes that my baby girl had to witness and experience this horror.

I spent three very long months in this hospital. I underwent sixteen operations and more pain than any human being should ever have to endure. Due to several fractures, my leg was held together with external fixators (metal bars that went right through my bones in several areas) and then it was suspended in mid-air with long gauze strips that attached to a trapeze bar above me. I was flat on my back for three months in this one position. Thank goodness I was placed on an air-mattress to reduce the chance of getting bed sores.

In repeated operations, they took skin grafts from my thighs and placed them on my leg, only to have the skin become necrotic (the skin did not survive) and need to be debrided (another operation to remove the dead and unhealthy skin). This happened over and over until my thighs just bled and my nerve endings felt like I was on fire.

Every morning, eight plastic surgery residents showed up at my bedside to change the bandages, only to find that there had not been enough lubricant applied to this area, and so the bandages were stuck to my leg. At 6:00 a.m. like clockwork, they would rip off the bandages along with my skin. The gut-wrenching screams that would come from deep down in my soul did not seem to affect them. It was as though all they could see was my leg and had zero ability to see ME! You would have thought my leg and I were separate entities from each other. It was inhumane. The residents rotated every four weeks, so we are actually talking about 24 doctors in all. I believe this is where I began to lose my faith in this hospital and in the doctors.

In one of the operations, they removed part of the latissimus dorsi (the large muscle from my back) and put it on my foot, in an attempt to form a new heel for me, as mine had been ripped off by the impact of the wheel of the bus rolling over my leg.

My normal body weight at that time was around 130-135 pounds. Before I knew it, I was down to 90 pounds and my nutritional values were undetectable. After three months one of the main doctors called for a family meeting in my room where he began engaging with my family (as though I wasn't lying on the bed in front of him) and informed them that I would require a feeding tube in order for me to survive. It was at this moment that I turned to my former husband and said out loud, for the first time, "If you let them put a feeding tube in me, kiss me goodbye."

In all this time, for some reason, I had never feared for my life, but now, this was it, this was that moment! I just didn't have anything left to fight with. The doctor looked at me for the first time and said, "What would you like me to do?"

I asked him to please get me off the morphine, as I believed it was the immense amount of medication that was ultimately stopping me from wanting to eat. He did so, and within hours my head cleared, the morphine fog had lifted, and I was staring at what used to be my leg with clear eyes for the first time in months. I was horrified at what I saw. I looked at Marissa and said, "Good Lord, what are they doing? There isn't enough leg here to save." My leg had deteriorated so badly that I was looking at bone with skin hanging off of it. Nothing was intact, nothing was sustainable, and I did not believe I would ever walk again (at least not on this remnant of my leg).

While I respected the fact that I had voiced on several occasions that I did not want to lose my leg, by this point it would have been good for the doctors to have been honest and to have told me it was either me or my leg. I had now completely lost my faith in the doctors at this hospital. They had wanted so desperately to save my leg, but in the interim, they were losing ME.

I remember one night talking with Marissa and somehow the subject of amputation came up and she said "You know mom, it wouldn't be the worst thing in the world. You would finally be able to come home and begin to heal."

I don't remember the entire conversation about a potential amputation, but Marissa recently told me that I was completely despondent for 24 hours. I just stared out the window and would not talk to anyone. I guess I needed time to contemplate this un-imaginable decision and somehow face my deepest fears.

I do remember finally coming to the realization that if I ever wanted to go home, this part of my leg needed to come off. I had no idea what my life would look like, but I was very aware of the alternative. I had, in addition, instantly decided that I did not want to have the amputation done at this teaching hospital where there had been too many instances where I was not happy with my care.

I knew of a doctor that was the head of orthopedics in a private hospital (also in NYC) and within a few days, I was able to be transferred there. The Monday after Thanksgiving I became a left below knee amputee. Talk about giving thanks and seeing my blessings. Instead of devastation, I was so grateful to have this second chance, no matter what it looked like.

I was blessed that the orthopedist decided to ask a plastic surgeon to join him for my surgery, because together they were able to save my knee using the muscle that was originally intended for my heel. I stayed at the hospital for an additional two weeks to do some rehab and prepare to go home, and on December 16, 2005, I CAME HOME! Four very long and traumatic months were finally over!

Marissa chose not to go to China that semester and instead became my constant companion and main caretaker. Along with my former husband and my precious 16-year-old son David by my side, my true healing journey began.

I had stitches and staples in my residual limb (what was left of my left limb). I don't ever use the word stump. I was either on the couch or in a wheelchair. I was feeling so frail and weak and frightened. I couldn't walk (yet), I couldn't shower alone (yet), and I had to navigate getting upstairs to my bedroom on my butt.

Most people who are involved in such a serious incident do not survive. Why and how did I? The only thing I know for sure is that I was grateful to be alive.

When I think back to those days in the hospital, and when I first returned home, when my strength was all but gone, when the last thing I wanted was to get out of that bed, I had become acutely "aware" of an energy, a feeling, a voice that was not audible but ever present in my mind. It said, "Get up, you've got this, I've got you!"

This voice pushed me literally, one step at a time. It was a gut feeling that let me know very clearly that I needed to dig deep inside of myself. I suddenly knew that I wasn't alone. It was with me. It has always been with me. I found myself wanting to be in touch with this "awareness" more and more. It held onto me as I grabbed the walker for the first time and began my daily hopping: first ten feet, then a lap around the hospital floor.

I remember the first time I got up and hopped past the mirror in my room, I almost fainted. I looked like an emaciated little old lady. I couldn't believe this was me. I had a long road ahead of me for sure.

Three weeks after I arrived home, I had an appointment with a prosthetist to get my first leg. It was there that my true spiritual awakening began, with a woman by the name of Cheryl. She was my first teacher. My introduction. My G-D-send. My angel here on earth.

She sat with me for hours and spoke to me about things like going with the flow and possibly finding meaning in what I had been through. She strongly encouraged me to begin making a gratitude list every day. She encouraged me to focus on all the things I COULD do, instead of contemplating all the things I thought I'd never do. She put me in a mindset to keep moving forward. I was so grateful for her support. It made me want to walk and maybe even run. My first goal after getting home was to one day be able to walk my dog around the block. It took me months, but I did it.

As I kept my heart and my mind open, different opportunities began to appear. I was introduced to a retreat held in the Bahamas and I bravely made the choice to go.

It was one of the most amazing experiences of my life. Every day, we were offered the opportunity to go out on a beautiful catamaran into the deep blue waters of the Caribbean and swim with dolphins in the wild! I had learned to snorkel with just one fin, and I don't think anyone on board expected me to do the unthinkable. I got into that water and swam like a fierce force of nature. There was no stopping me. The dolphins were, by far, the most beautiful, loving, and peaceful beings I have ever encountered. It was a joy that is hard to describe, like something had touched my heart and it instantly burst open. I had been through so much, and I swear those dolphins brought me back to life.

This particular week was run by a very wonderful couple: Lou Corleto and Lydie Ometto. I am so grateful to the both of them for teaching me skills that have profoundly changed my life.

This was the first time that anyone had encouraged me to get rid of all the things that no longer served me. They suggested that I could actually delete any and all the negative information I had been given in the past, and that I could instead discover what would enhance me, my heart and my soul. I could start over with a "clean slate." I no longer held onto the ideas of how things "should" be and realized that everything that happens really does happen for a reason. These are all life lessons and challenges that encourage us to grow. I decided to become a victor instead of a victim.

Instead of saying, "Look what happened to me," I began wondering, "What could I do with this?" Changing my attitude and my focus has been a game changer for me. It's kind of funny because if you ask me how I feel about that dreadful day, I would tell you that, reflecting back, it felt like I was wiped out and given a "clean slate." A new beginning. A second chance. I could, and would, do things differently. We arrive here on this Earth as pure and innocent beings, and within minutes, expectations are put on us. We quickly forget who we are.

We have so many experiences that shape and mold who we become. I have learned that my life is a journey back to who I was before everyone else told me who I needed to be. This wasn't an accident. There are no accidents. This was an opportunity for me to start over. I was given a second chance to experience life on my own terms; not my mother's, not my former husband's, not my schoolteachers, certainly not my sisters or anyone else in my life that had an influence over me.

I don't dwell on what I have lost. Instead, I put my energy into the things and the people that support and love me. I learned to count on myself. I learned to trust my body simply by deciding to be grateful for it. Look at what this body has carried me through. Instead of looking at what may be perceived as imperfect, I now see a strong healthy body that is my ride or die.

I returned to yoga after taking a three-year hiatus to heal, and I have added meditation and Pilates to keep me centered and balanced. I go dancing as often as I can and dance my butt off like no one else's business. I became a volunteer peer visitor for new amputees, which is so rewarding and healing for me. I had a peer visitor right before my amputation, and this woman gave me so much hope that I am now honored to do the same for others. I also find that the best medicine for me when I get down (yes, it happens occasionally) is to turn my attention away from myself and be there for someone else. This is the real reason I think we are all here: to help each other through our journeys. Everyone goes through difficult and challenging times in their life. It is ultimately up to us to decide what to do with those challenges. I choose to be positive. I choose to keep this spiritual awareness close, in my heart.

When I open my eyes and look down to the place where the rest of my leg used to be, instead of feeling sorry for myself, I remember to be grateful. Grateful that I am still here, enjoying my life to the fullest. I travel whenever I get the chance. I swim. I snorkel. I have ziplined in Alaska. I have gone skydiving in Tennessee. I have ridden a camel in Israel. Nothing will stop me from living my best life. This source energy gave me the strength to get out of an unhealthy marriage. It has given me the courage to sell my home and move to another state to be closer to my daughter and her family. I am able to travel to Florida once a month to visit my son and his family. I have the cutest and sweetest grandkids I could ever have imagined, and I am still here to enjoy it all!

If you are going through something challenging, I hope you remember that we all have this inner loving source energy. It is simply a part of you. I have leaned into it and learned to accept and embrace life with all of its ups and downs. It gives me the freedom to be angry, sad, disappointed, or even depressed, and to get back up and start again. It is simply a more peaceful way of living. As long as I believe it, and as long as I allow myself to feel its presence, I know I'll always be okay.

About Shari Dobrin Caradonna, PTA

Shari is a dynamic force of nature, and a retired Certified Physical Therapist Assistant with 26 years of experience. Hailing from the vibrant shores of Long Island, New York, her passion for dancing and yoga has resonated and stayed with her throughout her life. Shari's journey took an unexpected turn when tragedy threatened to take away her ability to enjoy those passions. Instead of succumbing to despair, she embraced the challenge, connecting with her inner spirit and the support of like-minded souls. This transformative experience brought out her resilience and ignited her determination to live a life overflowing with gratitude and joy.

Her two children and their families are her greatest source of motivation. Shari's story is a testament to the power of perspective, proving that true strength often emerges when we least expect it. With every step, she inspires others to open their hearts and minds, reminding us all that life's challenges can lead to profound growth and fulfillment. Shari currently

Shari Dobrin Caradonna, PTA resides in New Jersey with her miniature goldendoodle and fully embraces the profound happiness of spending time with her kids and grandkids.

You can reach out to Shari at: Budda2345@aol.com

For a free bonus chapter please go to:
www.wattpad.com/user/Scaradon

Chapter 2

Unstoppable Elfie: A Journey of Choice and Resilience

Elfie Knecht

It is January 1st. The beginning of a new year. I wake up groggy in the intensive care unit (ICU) of the hospital I was born in. Why am I here? What has happened? How did I get here? The attending nurse tells me I was brought to the emergency room on the morning of December 31st as a trauma victim.

I begin to assemble the pieces of this puzzle during the next few hours. I learn that I am the victim of a motor vehicle accident. While crossing the street at a stop sign as a pedestrian, I was struck by an unlicensed driver in a vehicle at the intersection and pinned between it and a second vehicle. The result: amputation of my left leg below the knee, and my right leg was crushed.

My advent on Planet Earth began at this same hospital. I was born into a fundamentalist family with parents who had emigrated from Germany and experienced deep trauma from WWII. I was their firstborn child, their pride and joy. My sister was born four years later, followed by three more siblings in the subsequent 11 years. The initial doting I had experienced shifted. I was expected to co-parent my two brothers and two sisters in adult ways: cooking, folding laundry, doing dishes, cleaning. Practicing our respective musical instruments and doing homework were part of the order of every day.

Our childhood was focused on attending church services, Sunday school, prayer meetings and singing in the children's choir. A militaristic regimen was superimposed on my childhood. There was no free time to rest or play, read a book, or simply be a child. I was not permitted to function as an individual and had no autonomy.

My parents, as authoritarian adults, harshly dictated every move and did not permit us to voice any opinions. To ensure compliance, my father carried a literal "big stick" which he used to discipline us. He was cruel, and both physically and verbally abusive to me, his eldest daughter. His war survival mentality did not allow for any kindness or softness with his children. His assessment of me was likely that I was opinionated and asked too many questions. He and my narcissistic mother always told me: "The time will come for you to do what you want, and make decisions for yourself, when you are 18 years old."

Precisely at 18 years and one month, my father took my house key and carried my few boxes of belongings to the front door. My mother watched as he set them on the street curb in the rain. They definitively stated that God had spoken to them, indicating "it was time."

I spent the next weeks frantically seeking shelter, trying to find a landlord who would allow an 18-year-old who looked 12 to sign a lease. A friend's mom vouched for my ability to pay rent, since I had a full-time job, and I moved into a studio apartment with only the clothes on my back. Friends came to the rescue with necessities: a small cot to sleep on, towels, a blanket, pillow, some dishes and utensils, along with a small table and two folding chairs. My independence began to blossom away from my family, as did my "fuck you" attitude. My resilience took root.

Then, two years later, at 20 years old, after being on my own both physically and financially, my life changed drastically and irreparably when I found myself on a bed in the ICU, immobilized. I learned that I had lost so much blood, I was close to dying.

During that long day... into night... into the first day of a brand-new year, I left my body. I fell in and out of consciousness. A visceral out-of-body experience I had in this liminal space clearly delineated the choices I had before me. I saw two rooms. In the room on the left, I noticed it was dark and dingy. The blinds were drawn. There was no light. No humans. Not a single soul was present to interact with. Silence hung heavy in the air. "How depressing," I remember thinking. I entered the room on the right and was surprised and shocked. The energy inside was palpable. A party was in progress. Dancing, singing and pulsating rhythm filled the space. The sun poured through the windows. Fluid conversations permeated the room. I stepped into the center of the room. At that moment, the message I distinctly heard was: "CHOOSE. Choose your life."

No delay for me. The choice was crystal clear. A life of light, fun and possibility with many friends and humans of all nationalities, creeds, tribes, sizes, ages and shapes is what I definitively chose for myself in that moment, there in that out-of-body space of the subconscious. That pivotal moment set the tone for what has become a life of adventure while navigating life's challenges.

The next four months were spent in the hospital, followed by many months of physical therapy to regain my mobility and strength. Since my right leg had been crushed, I was in a full-leg cast for 10 months. I could not have a prosthesis (an artificial leg) made for my left leg until more healing occurred. Numerous surgeries ensued ~ to give me more mobility.

At 20 years old, my world had seemingly come to a screeching halt and my independence was nonexistent.

My injuries were so severe, I was unable to work for four years. The shadow of anger and despondency hung over me like a thick cloud. Why was it taking so long to recuperate and resume my life? How could my family, who say they love their god, not be supportive to their daughter and sister? Why did I feel so much physical, emotional, psychological, spiritual and psychic pain?

At the same time, I was absolutely clear that I had chosen life. I now had the freedom to make decisions apart from my parents. I had survived my childhood and could now implement the courage to thrive. I was resolute in my clear-cut choice to be fully present to my new life. After several years, I visited a prosthetist who fabricated my very first prosthesis, an artificial leg that allowed me to take my first steps back to normalcy. I began to recognize the need for rest and pure fun while resuming daily life and tasks. My childhood had required me to function as an adult. Now, as an adult, I allowed myself to explore my desires with gusto and play with abandon as a child would.

Taking a flying trapeze class was a fantastical desire that I turned into reality when I found a suitable outdoor location. I had to climb a rope ladder to reach the trapeze, which required unanticipated energy. My vertigo left me feeling dizzy. I kept my prosthesis on to climb the ladder, then removed it to transition to the trapeze. How delightful is the memory of that *whoosh* of swinging, of flying through air and space in time, then hanging from the trapeze bar.

Choosing life in every *whoosh* while allowing for untethered enjoyment. I let go of the trapeze bar and dropped to the net below. My prosthesis followed, released by the assistant above. I reattached it and lowered myself to the ground. Still floating from the experience, I walked away, all body parts fully intact.

As my perception of opportunities expanded, activities that had felt like limitations when I had first become an amputee now presented themselves as enticing possibilities to explore.

My next adventure was tandem skydiving, with an instructor strapped to my back. To prevent my prosthesis from falling off at an altitude of 12,000 feet, I taped it firmly to my body. Ready, set, go!! My weightless body moved effortlessly through the air, at a speed of 120 miles per hour. In those two minutes of freefall, I experienced an eternity of intense movement sans constriction ~ only expanse. The freedom to just be me. When my descent slowed, I opened the parachute of my life with a bird's-eye view to the wonder and choices available to me. We landed safely on the landing strip. The skydive mimicking life.

These astounding moments in the air solidified for my future life that, though filled with challenges, some trepidation, and many un-knowns, I am unstoppable.

So, I started my own business as a licensed New York City tour guide and travel coordinator. My strong organizational and planning skills served me well in this gratifying and satisfying endeavor. I had extensive knowledge of the city I live in and love, thus being able to share its nuance with visiting tourists. I offered guided tours in both English and German, and shorter tours in Spanish. The most exciting part of being a tour guide, for me, was the opportunity to converse for hours with the most interesting humans from all corners of the globe. Communication and connection always happened, even when our languages were different.

One weekend I decided to go swimming, an activity I had not yet participated in as an amputee. I purchased a waterproof cover for my new prosthesis to enable submersion in the water without damaging the hardware of my prosthesis. Wearing my brand-new royal blue swimsuit, I walked bold and proud into the Atlantic Ocean. What a memorable experience!! I have repeated it many times since then, though the swimsuit size has changed periodically.

Recognizing and stepping into my power, I formed an amputee support group that met monthly at a local hospital. Our mission was to provide hope, support and information to fellow leg and arm amputees. For several years, a co-facilitator and I did outreach in our amputee community. All amputee attendees were invited to share their struggles, joys and accomplishments in a safe space and supportive environment. This was a rewarding experience for me.

During this time, our amputee group received an email from a choreographer whose integrated dance company was looking for dancers with disabilities.

Incredulous, I responded. A two-year relationship which incorporated dance movement into my life began. I am incredibly grateful for the opportunity offered me by this well-known and talented choreographer. I learned so much about the ways my mind restricts and precludes me from trying before starting. I learned to trust my body more and gave myself permission to expand my own imposed limits on my physical body. This gift continues to surprise me. Thus was ushered in a more unstoppable era of my life.

Then, it was time for a bigger adventure. I had met another kind, loving and lovable soul whose appetite for adventure superseded mine. We married and traveled to Hawaii for our honeymoon. Walking extensively, hiking, and attempting to dance hula were some of the challenges I faced there as an amputee. I always felt supported by my new sweetheart. When my beautiful partner said, "let's go ziplining," my heart began to pound while my chest heaved. In allowing my fear and anxiety to coexist with desire and new possibility, I also had to contend with my acrophobia (my fear of heights) and vertigo.

Additionally, the very real concern of losing my prosthesis at these heights came into focus. As with skydiving, I vigorously taped my prosthesis to my body before we began our nine zips, each higher and longer than the previous one. The cables connected us from valley to hill and beyond. Our harnesses were attached to a pulley system, and we wore helmets for our safety. The thrill and height of the zips allowed us to enjoy nature from a bird's perspective, while combining the rush of flying with the serenity of the outdoors. Best of all, it was an adventure we shared together.

While seeking out new adventures, I continued to tend to my personal needs, periodically having a new prosthesis made. The updated technologies available to us as amputees allowed for a smoother gait, a more integrated step, less energy expenditure and the ability to walk more effortlessly on an incline or decline. A new prosthesis increased my functional living and improved the quality of my life. It also allowed me to be more active and unstoppable. Unstoppable Elfie, quite literally, at work.

All appeared to be well when I arrived at the juncture of 36 years as an amputee and 56 years on planet Earth, with a figurative view of the rearview mirror of my life.

Then, over a period of many months, I noticed an unresolved blister on the left side of my tongue. I thought I had burned my tongue. Over time, my left tongue became raw and inflamed, as if someone had razored across the surface. Eating and swallowing became almost impossible, and I began to consume liquid shakes for nutrition, using a straw. I hoped the pain and this new nightmare would resolve. It did not, and I was compelled to act.

In 2020, during COVID, I was diagnosed with tongue cancer, a mouth cancer that, for me, is likely the result of an autoimmune condition known as oral lichen planus (OLP). My left tongue biopsy was identified as squamous cell carcinoma. This is one of many possible oral cancers.

The recommended surgery was a partial glossectomy, described plainly as partial removal of my left tongue. The thought of how this would impact my ability to chew and swallow was devastating. The knowledge that my speech could be eradicated or severely altered was terrifying. I am an articulate, verbose and loquacious multilingual conversationalist by nature. How could I continue as a tour guide? Additionally, I felt the stark and jarring contrast of being a figurative tourist in my own life and this unpredictable new landscape. With much trepidation, in tandem with great hope, I embarked on the journey through this surgery.

The surgery was unsuccessful, and my oral cancer returned several months later. I sought out and met with a world-renowned ENT surgeon whose expertise matched his humanity. He recommended a second partial glossectomy and the removal of a portion of my left lymph nodes, known as left neck dissection. My fear of the unknown prevailed. I chose not to have this surgery, opting instead to explore other therapies, which were only temporarily successful.

Increased pain levels and an ongoing diet of liquid nutrition dictated that I implement another difficult choice. Yet again, I found myself angry and despondent. The real possibility that I would not be able to communicate with comprehensive verbal speech held me in its vice grip. The knowledge that my taste buds and ability to eat could be severely affected filled me with anxiety.

A tumultuous and life-altering experience ensued.

In March 2023, at 58 ½ years of age, I elected to have a second partial glossectomy with neck dissection, followed by six weeks of radiation, 30 treatments in total. This was absolutely the most challenging time of my almost six decades on planet Earth. During every detail of this difficult life chapter, I felt the balm of care and kindness my partner offered, including unwavering support.

After surgery, I continued a liquid diet for many months, attempting to maintain minimal weight loss. Difficulty swallowing, known as dysphagia, was a constant, consistent and unwelcome aspect of my oral cancer journey. For many months I had to sleep upright, so I could accomplish the very basic function of swallowing, one I have always taken for granted.

My ability to taste food was significantly compromised. A juicy burger, macaroni and cheese, or a delicious tomato sauce all tasted like cardboard. Chocolate tasted like mud. As a huge foodie and self-proclaimed gourmet cook, I faced the shocking reality of having no viable taste buds, which remain limited, even now. A dry mouth and lack of saliva, known as xerostomia, persist to this day. A water bottle is my constant companion, to assist with any cough resulting from mouth dryness. Most recently, fibrosis, a thickening of the scar tissue in my mouth and on the exterior of my neck has appeared, a result of radiation therapy.

At times, then and even now, my deep and wide grief resurfaces. A heavy cloud. A hill that becomes a mountain. A grief for the part of my oral cancer journey that is a constant and consistent reality. MY reality. No way to turn away from it, no way to mask it, and no way to sugarcoat it.

When it descends like a heavy fog, I return to the remembrance of my choice of life, my courage to choose to live fully, which has remained with me since my amputation. It is also where I am able to acknowledge the huge support I received and continue to receive from friends, globally and locally. This is inextricably linked to my healing journey. Friends have shown up for me in amazing and unanticipated ways: via letters and gifts mailed; phone calls; texts; emails; gorgeous and aromatic flower bouquets delivered; even balloon bouquets. Their constant and consistent kindness and compassion is invaluable. For this great gift of friendship, I have a universe of gratitude.

And then there is the depth of unconditional love that was and continues to be shared willingly and openly by my life partner of 17 years. In every instance and at every stage of my developing oral cancer journey, my partner embraced the indispensable role of providing unwavering and crucial support in all forms, which enhanced my physical healing.

The unkindness and cruelty doled out in gobs by my parents was replaced with my partner's softness and sweetness. I had never felt this before. The war burden that had been imprinted on me from my family and previous generations began to liquefy. The embrace of love, understanding and acceptance freely given by my partner allowed me to relax more fully, to rest. Cancer requires rest to heal. The love also allowed for healing to begin. Healing from my childhood. My gratitude for my sweetheart, the love of my life, is boundless.

Inside this conversation of healing, my resilience flourished, enhanced by my consistent "fuck you" attitude, which engendered my survival. I was determined to regain the ability to have comprehensive verbal speech.

Post-operatively, my speech-language pathologist and I worked together extensively on my articulation, resonance, fluency, and pronunciation, as well as swallowing. The tongue is a muscle that requires daily exercise. One such suggested exercise includes licking my lips, over and over, in a complete 360-degree circle, both clockwise and counterclockwise. Another requires slowly stretching my tongue to both left and right cheeks inside my mouth repeatedly for two minutes several times every day. Speaking aloud continuously requires an energy most people take for granted. Verbal communication, for me, requires careful management of my time and anticipated daily activity. It also requires focus, so I can be clear and clearly understood. In all aspects, the deep-rooted knowledge that I am unstoppable prevails. I continue to choose life in every moment.

As a tour guide, I recalled the meticulous planning I had employed with every tour group I had worked with. Now, that forethought is necessarily reserved for me. This allows me to be more keenly aware of the gift of each present moment as I move through this circuitous and ongoing cancer journey. Compassion for myself is another important ingredient. I am more deeply engaged with my life daily, with copious ladles of gratitude.

In anticipation of my recent milestone birthday, I made a list of adventures I want to experience in my new decade. On my actual birthday, I enjoyed a gratifying hour of axe throwing, which boosted both my mental and physical vitality, as promised. What a powerful release of excess frustration and grief I experienced!! Also recognizable was my renewed energy and stamina, 18 months post-surgery and radiation treatment. It was indeed a HAPPY and unstoppable birthday for Unstoppable Elfie.

Empowered, I planned another long-awaited and much-deliberated adventure: rock climbing. Rock climbing is my most exciting adventure since my 2020 tongue cancer diagnosis. Stamina and endurance are requisite components for this ambitious activity. In 2023, I could not have imagined this outcome. At an indoor facility, I climbed 30 feet (9 meters) of a 45-foot (14-meter) wall in three persistent tries. My instructor was dynamic and patient. I experienced a level of euphoria heretofore unidentified. My time on the wall was, quite literally, a proverbial "two steps forward and one step back" or no movement at all. Then, I had to attempt alternate approaches on the wall in my journey to new heights. What a metaphor for life. The rock climb of my life, and all of ours.

I continue to reach for, and figuratively taste, all the fruits of my life disguised as adventures in all moments, employing the boundless energy and stamina that my new body allows, along with fortitude, hope, perseverance, resilience, courage, and a necessary dose of compassion for myself.

I AM UNSTOPPABLE ELFIE!

About Elfie Knecht

Elfie is a spirited and adventurous human with a passion for bringing people together. As an independent and multilingual licensed New York City tour guide, she creates unforgettable experiences for visitors from around the globe.

Known for her sassy demeanor, warm smile, and boundless energy, she thrives on connection ~ whether hosting lively house parties or guiding groups through the vibrant streets of New York City.

Elfie finds joy in playing the piano and accordion, and she dances as a way to express her love for movement and life.

Elfie's journey has been shaped by two life-altering experiences: one traumatic, the other unforeseen and devastating. Both brought her to the brink of death. Elfie's resilience, perseverance, connection to others and compassion for herself were pivotal to her healing process.

Now she celebrates life with laughter, music, and adventure, sharing her indomitable spirit and zest with everyone she meets. Joy is her essence. Fun is her mantra. Profound gratitude is her song.

For your "I am Unstoppable" Guide, email Unstoppable Elfie at: elfiek59@gmail.com

Chapter 3

ROSARIES OF RESILIENCE: FROM GENOCIDE TO RITUAL

Sharokin BetGevargiz

THE FALLEN TREE AND DAMASCUS ROSES

Hurricane Helene's misleading forecasts quickly converted to a cacophony of tornado sirens blasting our phones late into the night. Yet my 89-year-old mother was unfazed. "Nothing will happen." Her stubbornness matched the ancient water laurel just 10 feet from our home ~ a tree whose roots had defied decades of storms, clinging to life despite its hollow core.

Kneeling at the bedroom window overlooking the towering laurel, I surrendered to The Great Spirit and I whispered a prayer. I summoned my ancestral guardians from the Mesopotamian Pantheon: Inanna, Ishtar, Enheduanna and Adad. I called on my father's spirit. "If tonight is the night you fall," I whispered to the tree, my voice shaking, "fall away from us. Protect us one last time."

My partner left to check his house nearby. I huddled in my mother's walk-in closet, pleading with her to join me, but she refused. At 2:30 a.m. a pounding on the door jolted me awake. My partner's panicked voice cut through the storm. "The tree fell!"

We had not heard the crash. I was wearing earplugs, and my mother is hard-of-hearing. Racing outside, I braced against the wind and rain. The massive tree had fallen just as I'd prayed, its limbs stretching harmlessly across the fence line. Miraculously, neither our house nor the neighbor's bore its weight.

THE AFTERMATH

Neighbors ventured out with flashlights, the storm raging, their faces pale against the eerie glow of the rain. The sprawling branches resembled the aftermath of a battlefield, raw and devastating. My mother stood in the doorway; her shawl clutched tightly around her shoulders. "It's a miracle," she murmured, her voice trembling with awe.

The tree lay exposed, its hollow center revealing the hidden years of decay. It felt like a death in the family ~ a quiet witness to our lives, suddenly gone.

Without power, the heat and humidity were unbearable for my elderly mom. We evacuated to a hotel for three nights. When we returned to meet the arborist, the house remained sweltering and oppressive, the air still heavy with the storm's tension. The arborist confirmed the tree was one of the largest he'd seen felled by Helene.

RITUAL UNDER THE TREE

Days later, I stood beneath the massive roots of the fallen tree. Once towering over our home, it symbolized my family's resilience. Now, lying on earth, it stood as a silent testament to survival despite unseen wounds. Here, where the tree fell, I sensed a portal opening ~ a gateway inviting me to ground myself and embrace a new beginning.

This grounding became an offering of gratitude ~ releasing heavy energies and welcoming renewal. I was called to do a ritual with my Mesa, a sacred cloth bundle with rocks used as an altar for shamanic practices. A shaman who carries a Mesa has walked the medicine wheel, confronting their wounds, shadows, and weaknesses to hold space for others' healing.

I sat at the base of the fallen tree with my Mesa open, grounding in gratitude, releasing heavy energies, and calling for renewal. I used a rattle and seven Kipa ~ sacred rocks representing the chakras ~ to perform a Transition Spiral ritual, releasing the tree's energy.

This ritual was for Native ancestors of this land, the descendants of the enslaved, my father's spirit in the garden, and my mother's enduring resilience. It was also for my Assyrian ancestors, whose survival and strength resonate deeply within me.

THE ROOTS OF RESISTANCE

For more than 6,000 years, the Assyrians, one of the world's earliest civilizations, flourished in Beth Nahrain ~ the land between the Tigris and Euphrates Rivers, now modern-day Iraq. As pioneers of writing, astronomy, and governance, we shaped the foundations of human progress. Today, Assyria no longer exists as a country. We are a stateless people, scattered across the Middle East, with most now living abroad in exile. Promised safe havens after the fall of the Ottoman Empire, we instead faced betrayal, displacement, and near erasure. Only a few Assyrians remain in their ancestral homeland.

Two-thirds of the Assyrian population perished during the Seyfo Genocide of World War I, perpetrated by the Muslim-led Ottoman Empire and Kurdish forces. Alongside Armenians and Greeks, Assyrians ~ ancient Orthodox Christians from the Middle East ~ suffered mass killings, forced deportations, and cultural annihilation. Assyrians are among the earliest Christian communities, tracing our faith to the apostles and maintaining liturgical traditions in Aramaic, the language of Christ.

Raphael Lemkin, the Polish-Jewish lawyer who coined the term genocide, cited the 1933 Assyrian Simmele massacre as a vivid example of how genocide devastates a people, highlighting its systematic destruction and lasting impact.

Despite these horrors, the Assyrian spirit endures. Though our ancient language is endangered, there is hope. My brother's daughters recently traveled to Iraq, reconnecting with their heritage and renewing their commitment to preserve our traditions. Their journey reflects our resilience, showing that survival is an ongoing, active choice.

THE ROOTS OF RESILIENCE AND DEVOTION

Resilience flows through my family, much like the lifeblood of my mother's 300 Damascus rose bushes, all rooted from a single stem brought from Iran. These roses thrived in Connecticut's harsh winters, marking summer's arrival with their fragrance. Each year, their petals became rosewater, jam, hydrosols, and rosaries ~ ritual offerings infused with prayer and intention.

Rosaries embody devotion, connecting generations to the sacred. Ancient flower garlands, offered to honor The Mother ~ Earth, the Divine Feminine, Inanna ~ symbolized life's cycles and grounded prayers in nature. These evolved into prayer bead traditions across cultures, from Buddhist meditation to Catholic rosaries, enduring resistance. Like Enheduanna's hymns to Inanna, the rosary is a ritual of devotion, threading prayer and connection to the Divine Mother. For my sister and me, it has become a bridge to connect with our mom. While we speak of the Divine Feminine, her prayers to Mary are a quiet, subversive act of honoring the Great Mother within the Church.

Threading beads with my mother was sacred, tying us to the lineage of women before us. Healing is not linear but made of small, meaningful acts, strung like beads. Today, my sister and her daughters tend the roses, preserving their legacy. Like the roses, my family carried its roots across continents, surviving revolutions and dislocation. For my mother, each rose bush was a declaration: "We are still here."

As I prayed under a tree, I felt the weight of loss, broken promises, and the fragile future of my culture ~ a pain that feels like losing parts of yourself to history. Yet, I also felt the hope of my ancestors and others striving for peace. That ritual became a pledge to honor their legacy and a call for solidarity with all oppressed peoples.

ACTIVISM, FAITH, AND CONFRONTING SILENCE
HIGH SCHOOL LOVE AND BETRAYAL

In high school, I fell in love for the first time. He was tall, kind, and one year older, with a gentle laugh that lifted the silent weight I carried. But he was African American, so our relationship had to remain a secret, hidden beneath layers of shame and constructed lies.

As Middle Easterners, navigating forced assimilation into a system shaped by white privilege, we were taught to value lighter-skinned bodies over darker ones. Internalized racism reinforced these hierarchies, dictating not just how we saw ourselves but who we believed was "acceptable" to love. My family's fears left no room for love that defied their expectations.

When the relationship ended, it wasn't their disapproval that broke us but betrayal. One evening, I walked into a friend's dorm and found him lying across her lap. Though fully clothed, their intimacy shattered me.

That night, desperate to numb the pain, I swallowed a handful of ibuprofen pills ~ not to die, but as a cry for help. Stumbling into the rain, I collapsed on the grass, sobbing into the storm.

"All I wanted was to be held," I lamented, my voice lost in the downpour.

The ambulance arrived, its flashing lights slicing through the darkness as they lifted me onto the stretcher. I met his gaze one last time, the sting of betrayal still raw in my chest. But even that paled in comparison to the crushing shame of knowing my parents would find out.

Activism and Shattered Expectations

The day I transferred to the University of Vermont, I joined students protesting the Gulf War. The sharp January air carried chants against U.S. aggression in Iraq ~ the land of my ancestors. I became politicized, seeing my personal pain reflected in the world's injustices.

Activism became my lifeline, an outlet for the rage within me. I shaved my head, rejected societal norms, and poured myself into protests and organizing. My fury became a weapon against racism, sexism, war, and homophobia. But this passion came at a cost.

One night, two drunk white men hurled a glass bottle at our shantytown on the university green, shouting, "Illegal aliens! Go back where you came from!" The attack left us shaken. As a resident assistant, I trusted a campus officer during the investigation, but he twisted my words to fabricate a report. In this false account, I and others were accused of leading an outrageous act: burning white student's foreheads with the word "racist." This baseless narrative and racial scapegoating forced me to withdraw for an entire semester.

Generational Scars of Rage

My rage wasn't just about the injustices around me; it was deeply personal. It stemmed from boundaries violated in my youth, the silences forced upon my body, and the survival legacy of my ancestors. It carried the pain of generations: my grandmother, Mama Deena, who fled genocide on foot; her mother, Elishva, whose world was shattered in a single night; and Anna Badal, my mother's maternal aunt, whose life was forever marked by the Seyfo Genocide.

In 1914, Anna was an 18-year-old mother still bleeding from childbirth when the massacre reached the Assyrian village of Takeh-Ardeshy. Unable to flee, she stayed behind with her parents and newborn. That night, two Kurdish militia stormed their farmhouse, forcing Anna's father, Envia, to kneel with his neck on Elishva's lap before violently beheading him. The newborn's cries mixed with Elishva's screams as Anna was dragged away into the snow-covered night.

For eight months, Anna endured captivity, surviving through sheer will and resilience. When she returned, she found only devastation. Her daughter had died, her husband was mortally wounded, and her mother was lost to the chaos of war. Though Anna survived, her suffering didn't end. Rejected and ostracized by her community, she left to rebuild her life elsewhere.

Anna's story reflects the enduring scars carried by Assyrian women whose family wounds are etched into our lineage.

THE FAMILY SECRET AND STRUGGLE FOR BELONGING

Loyalty defined our family. Love meant holding tightly to each other, even when it hurt. My mother and her sister, bound by shared sacrifices and unspoken expectations, married brothers ~ a pairing meant to keep the family close but with little room for boundaries. My aunt, the elder, leaned on my father as a father figure to her children while her husband worked abroad. In this setup, loyalty often meant silently accepting crossed boundaries, bearing burdens without complaint, and equating love with self-sacrifice and quiet endurance ~ frequently at the cost of emotional well-being.

As my sister and I grew, we inherited this silence ~ a loyalty held in looks, gestures, and actions but rarely in words. The price of this unexpressed pain stretched our bonds even as it tied us tighter. Family secrets haunted the spaces between us, unspoken but palpable.

I questioned everything, including compulsory heterosexuality, and identified as queer ~ a truth my family couldn't accept. My sister's sharp words on a call still sting: "What else will you do to shock the family?" She blamed my first love for my reluctance to be with men.

Her accusation pierced me, but I found the courage to speak a deeper truth. Trembling, I revealed I had been sexually violated by someone we both knew. Her silence was deafening. She didn't ask for details. She knew. After the call, I sat alone, holding the weight of everything unsaid but sensing the faintest glimmer of hope. Speaking my truth, even in whispers, planted a seed ~ a step toward healing.

A Sister's Dream and a Turning Point

One night, she shared a dream of our grandmothers and great-grandmothers, their faces lined with wisdom and strength. In her dream, she wielded a sword, beheading the toxic patriarchy that had haunted generations of women, severing the cycles of violence and oppression. With powerful resolve, she envisioned our ancestors taking responsibility, healing the past, and transforming its blessings into a future of well-being for our future descendants.

Her dream became a shamanic metaphor for the healing we were undertaking to mend our family's wounds. I saw my role expand from activist and survivor to healer, storyteller, and bridge between the personal and collective. Together, we embraced our roles as co-guardians of our family's legacy, navigating caregiving, dynamics, and standing as pillars for each other.

Over time, my sister and I nurtured the seeds of our shared healing, transforming fractures into an unbreakable bond. Like the roses we tend, our bond has weathered conflict and loss, blooming stronger with time. Her strength mirrors the roots we share, grounding us in the enduring sisterhood and resilience.

CAREGIVING, BOUNDARIES, AND THE HEALING JOURNEY

THE WEIGHT OF CAREGIVING

Caregiving has become a meaningful way for me to spend time with my mom. I support her with errands, doctor visits, and Sunday Church outings. Among my friends, she's seen as an adopted mother and grandmother. As the oldest living ancestor in our family, she is stepping into her matriarch role. I am her advocate, translator, and companion. Though we see each other daily, she often says, "Come sit here. I never got to see you today." It's both heartwarming and exasperating.

Our evolving relationship has deepened our bond in unexpected ways. She remains independent but increasingly relies on me. One evening, after she dismissed my care suggestions, I said, "I love you, but I need to be heard too." Her softened gaze marked a shift.

Caregiving is an emotional preparation ~ a rite of passage. Her worries sometimes spill over into cleaning frenzies, unfinished tasks, or struggles with her eyesight. These moments remind me why her story matters and why it is essential to tell it now.

Generational Patterns and Cultural Expectations

In Assyrian culture, preserving our heritage and caregiving are sacred offerings in honoring elders. My mother inherited these roles, caring for her father in Tehran while managing her family. In recent years, she cared for my father, who struggled with dementia. Though my sister and her family assisted with his care, the final years and days were the most challenging ~ an unspoken sacrifice that weighed heaviest on my mother.

The implicit costs of caregiving have shaped our family. My mother never spoke of her exhaustion in caring for my father, using silence and her hands to endure ~ through lacework, cooking, her gardens, and prayers. Her legacy is one of duty and creating beauty as a means of survival.

For my mother, preserving our language and culture meant becoming the unofficial historian of our Connecticut community ~ archiving stories, teaching high schoolers the Assyrian language, and preserving rare books. Her devotion extended to hosting ceremonies and exhibiting her lacework art. The pillars of her faith are preserving Assyrian language and culture, loving unconditionally, and praying to something greater than ourselves with rosary beads worn smooth by her hands.

Healing Through Boundaries and Ritual

Creating rosaries from Damascus rose petals my mother had preserved was a profound ritual for both of us. Late one night, sitting by her side, I reflected on the balance caregiving demanded ~ navigating her needs while honoring my own. Healing came not in grand gestures but in shared rituals, embodying her motto: "little by little." Together, we turned dried Damascus rose petals into rosary beads, threading prayers into each one.

As we threaded beads, infusing them with prayers, I felt connected ~ not just to her but to the lineage of women before us. These acts reminded me that healing isn't linear but a collection of meaningful moments over and across time. With her hands, she survived genocide, revolution, and exile ~ always working, always creating, one step at a time. As she strung the beads, I felt peace.

The ritual reminded me that healing, like survival, is a journey of living day by day, little by little. The beads carry her legacy ~ hands that have known devastation and resilience, crafting beauty and prayer from loss and endurance.

THE VOICE OF ENHEDUANNA AND THE PATH TO RECLAMATION

ENHEDUANNA'S CALL TO SPEAK

On a moonlit night at my altar, surrounded by softly glowing candles, Enheduanna came to me ~ not as a vision, but as an undeniable presence. A Mesopotamian high priestess and daughter of King Sargon, who unified the Assyrian Empire around 2300 BCE, she was the first known author to sign her name ~ a woman daring to claim her voice in a world bent on erasing her. Long before Homer's *The Iliad*, Enheduanna used her hymns to exalt Inanna, the divine feminine, legitimize her father's reign, and inscribe her truths into history.

Her words, filled with rage and reverence, declared divine power unapologetically, transforming anger into something sacred. That night, her presence felt like a hand reaching through time, commanding me: "Speak. Write. Inscribe your truth into the world, even if the world resists."

For the first time, I saw my family's history of displacement, survival, and resilience clearly. Like Enheduanna, I realized my voice could both heal and fight. Her call ignited something within me ~ not just to honor her legacy but to reclaim my own voice.

Enheduanna taught me that words are weapons, shields, and bridges. Silence is no longer an option ~ for Palestine, for the silenced child I once was, and for the resilience within us all. Her legacy reminds us that to speak is to resist, and to resist is to heal.

In one shamanic journey, I envisioned her handing me a scroll etched with words of fire. "This is yours," she said. "Write it. Live it." That moment has become my guiding force. Enheduanna's presence has been tangible in these rituals. Her hymns to Inanna, filled with reverence and defiance, echo in my prayers, reminding me that the sacred is woven into everyday life, waiting to be recognized.

A Rose on Fire: Ritual as Reclamation
From Fallen Tree to Growing Flame

The fallen water laurel mirrored the resilience in my blood and the inevitability of transformation shaped by storms of trauma and silence. Standing beneath its massive roots, I prayed not just for survival but for renewal. That prayer became a seed for the flame that now burns within me. Just as I whispered to the tree that stormy night, I whisper to the child within me: "If tonight is the night you fall, fall gently, but rise again. Root yourself anew. Stand for what matters."

As I laid out the Kipa and performed the Transition Spiral, I was not just honoring what had fallen, I was calling forth what would rise. In that moment, my lineage, the earth, and the divine converged. I claimed my place as a bridge between worlds, weaving my ancestors' resilience into the fabric of my own healing.

Like my family's roses, scarred yet enduring, this ritual reminded me that survival alone isn't enough. The roses, now tended by my sister and nieces, bloom as a testament to our journey ~ uprooted yet thriving. Together, we've nurtured the Damascus roses, threading prayers into their petals and passing their legacy to the next generation.

My nieces, as bearers of our ancestral language, are raising the next generation of future ancestors with a new, inclusive, and expansive ethos. They carry forward not only our stories and traditions but also the wisdom of our farming and culinary practices, weaving them into a vision of resilience and growth.

CLAIMING MY VOICE, CLAIMING MY LEGACY

Through every storm, I have learned that my voice is my strongest root. Like the roses, I bloom where I am planted, transforming loss into life, pain into poetry, and resistance into resilience. Like Enheduanna, I've turned my rage into words, my words into hymns, and my hymns into actions that ripple beyond me.

The fire within me is not just mine alone. It is my mother's, who planted roses in exile and declared, "We are still here." It is my father's, who visits as a cardinal, a quiet reminder of resilience. And it is for the generations yet to come, who will find in these words a map for their own healing and their own blooming.

I do not know where the next storm will lead, but I know this: I will stand, rooted and unwavering, like the roses that survive frost. And when I fall, it will not be the end. It will be the scattering of seeds, a promise that from every loss, something new will bloom.

About Sharokin BetGevargiz

Sharokin BetGevargiz, known spiritually as "Ishtaro," is an author, artist, ceremonialist, teacher, and shamanic practitioner whose work bridges ancient wisdom with modern healing. An Assyrian born in Iran, she draws from her heritage as a descendant of Indigenous people who survived genocide, blending resilience with sacred practices to empower transformation. Sharokin spent over a decade as a university professor, teaching design and user experience mapping ~ expertise she now uses to guide clients through pivotal transitions and align their lives with their highest good.

A graduate of the Light Body School of Energy Medicine under Alberto Villoldo, she integrates shamanic traditions with modern practices to help individuals release trauma and connect with their inner beloved. Her work fosters self-love and builds new neural pathways through movement and gratitude.

She revives lost Mesopotamian traditions, offering spiritually curious clients tools to navigate today's anxiety-driven culture. Recognized for outstanding client satisfaction, Sharokin is documenting her mother's legacy of resilience and creativity through a biography and memoir. As the founder of Whirling Shaman, she inspires others to embrace the sacred feminine and their journeys of self-discovery.

Want to shed your story and free your wings?

Contact Sharokin at **sharokinb@gmail.com** for a complimentary consultation.

Learn more at **www.whirlingshaman.com** and on Instagram **@whirling_shaman**.

Chapter 4

Intergenerational Gifts Guide the Way

Sandi Goodwin, MA, ERYT-500

My grandmother's rolling pin makes its rhythmic sound, rolling to and fro, to and fro, then a pause with the soft *shoosh* of smoothing flour over pastry as she speaks into the tape recorder. The tinny sound of an early 80's era cassette recording plays the familiar sounds of my mother's mother ~ whom we called Clarabelle rather than Grandma ~ rolling out dough for cinnamon rolls as my older sister interviews her. Her midwestern accent and the clicking of her dentures punctuate her frequent laughter as she speaks, even of difficult things. In her late seventies, much of what she relates about her childhood memories and where she lived and such are known history to me, but the attitude and the joy of being and doing are what stays with me each time I listen to the well-worn cassette tape. And the thing she says that I remember and love the most is, "You know, I've really enjoyed my life. Even with all the hard parts and difficulties, I've really enjoyed my life." And she laughs. I can see her in my mind's eye, lips pulled back in a wide smile, mouth open, dentures on full display as she tips her head back and lets her laughter come from her belly. I can see her salt and pepper hair in its short granny coif, blue eyes sparkling with mischief ~ always sparkling with mischief ~ as her knobby arthritic hands keep moving. Roll to and fro, to and fro, sprinkle flour and roll to and fro, to and fro.

One of my son's famous sayings when he was about 8 years old was, "Yeah, I come from a long line of STRONG women." It was true. Clarabelle endured many hardships in her life, from her mother dying shortly after her birth, to raising 7 children during the depression after being abandoned by her husband. She persevered after losing her first grandson in Vietnam and her oldest son shortly after. But she rolled with life ~ maybe her rolling pin was the answer as she rolled out dough for noodles, cinnamon rolls and apple dumplings. She kept going, her ubiquitous tennis shoes earning her the nickname, "The little old lady in tennis shoes."

And my mother, Jane, also persevered and endured family conflict and emotional abuse. She was known for showing up with fierce energy and a can-do attitude. She always seemed to be wearing combat boots and a helmet. She was the one to call if you had a problem, and she would arrive like she was going into battle, charging ahead bravely to tackle whatever needed to be done. In reality, my mother was glamorous, wore high heels and had beautifully dyed, highlighted, and coiffed hair at all times. Her makeup was careful and understated. Her nails were always long and polished. She wore diamonds on her fingers and White Diamonds perfume on her body. She floated in a miasma of scent and strength. Always well put together, my mother loved clothes and earrings. When people met her for the first time, they would say things like, "She's like a president's wife! Or a movie star!" She was beautiful and tough, with piercing green eyes, a wide square face, and a strong, angular jawline that said, "Don't mess with me!" Indeed, her nickname in the family was "The Godfather." You didn't cross her, and you always wanted her in your corner.

Once, Mom told me about how she had hopped on the local bus and took it to the mall by herself ~ without a purse or any money ~ and bought a dress. She demanded they look up her account. "I'm 90 years old, and I have been shopping with you for 70 years!" And they did. She had a way of commanding people. She used to tell me that when she and my father had some rental properties in a rough part of town, he always sent her to collect the rent. And she always got it. She wasn't scared. She once went into a house where a bunch of men were drinking, and she said she told them she wasn't leaving until she got the rent. And she did. My nephew tells a story about having a flat tire and showing up to a Walmart Tire Center after they were closed and how Mom talked them into opening up to put a new tire on his car. Another time, she showed up when my husband and I were trying to get a loan to buy our first house. They had turned us down, but Mom talked to them for a short time, and we got the loan! She was a soldier alright, and one in strappy heels, a flattering dress, and put together to stop a clock!

It is true that my son came from a long line of strong women. But where Clarabelle laughed and rolled through life, Mom charged into battle with it, molding it to her will whenever possible. And thank goodness, because 21 years after his famous comment about coming from a long line of strong women, my son died in a motorcycle accident, which caused my world to come to a screeching halt. I was in shock. Barely functional. I stared out the window for hours. Sat on the couch. Forgot the main ingredient in everything I tried to cook. At first I tried to be strong. "No, you don't need to come," I told Mom at first. Shortly after, I called her back: "Please come." "Of course I am coming," she replied.

Mom helped me through each and every step along the way. She helped me go through my son's things, pack up his home, go to the bank, and settle his affairs. She was gentle with me. She got to know my son's two daughters, her great-grandchildren, much better, and became a regular part of their lives by moving to be near us. We healed by being a family. By making food, playing games, and making art and crafts. Being together. Four strong women spanning four generations.

A dear friend who had lost her father as a child told me that her father's mother was key to her connection with her father's memory, and that because her grandmother talked of her father often, reminiscing about him at every gathering, he remained alive in her memory. I decided that it would be my job to do that for my son's two girls. I imagined putting on my own combat boots and helmet to show up for them ~ to be strong for them like my mother was strong for me, and like my grandmother was for her family through the many hardships they faced. I'm sure that is what got me through those first few years and throughout the awful pain and grief of that time. I enjoyed the time with my mom and my grand-girls. We had fun! Spa days and sleepovers and sewing parties and craft projects, and mostly just hanging out eating candy from the little candy dishes she had all over her house.

If Mom and my family got me through the early days of grief after losing my son, it was Yoga that got me across the sea of despair in the years to come. My decade plus of regular asana and meditation practice were like potatoes in the larder when the famine came. In grief, I could no longer meditate. I didn't have the focus. My mind ran roughshod over my intentions, but I had the gift of being present. In my yoga practice and with my girls. I am convinced that all those years of practice carried me though, as did my faith in the teachings of Yoga that say that those who have passed are never really gone. That comforted me. It soothed me to think that he had learned the necessary lessons in this life that allowed him to be ready to move on, to be freed from the karma that this lifetime taught him. And that he was free from his suffering. He had struggled with his mental health and with addiction. He had a heart of gold, and would give it away to whoever needed it. He loved his partner and his girls to no end. We all missed him desperately, and we were there for each other, a closer family, perhaps because of it.

Because my yoga community knew of my loss, I became the go-to person when someone else experienced loss. My Restorative Yoga class became a de facto grief group. I created a grief workshop which turned into a weekly grief support circle that ended with some restorative poses. We did rituals. We lit candles.

We read aloud from inspiring works and shared our hearts, tears and laughter with one another. Again, I had others to be strong for. I made the connection that my grandmother, Clara, also lost a son and a grandson. My mother had many miscarriages, one far enough along that she could tell it was a boy. And so she, too, had lost in the same way. And they had carried on, rolling dough and donning combat boots and showing up with fierce determination, humor, and grace to help those who needed it.

Ten years on, it was my time to be strong for my mother. Alzheimer's was taking hold of her, and her independent living facility was making her move somewhere else, even though they had a memory care section. She was "too active," they said. And I could see that was the case. When equipped with a wristband that would lock the doors if she tried to leave, Mom ricocheted like a pinball from one exit to the next with her walker, getting madder and madder each time she was prevented from leaving. They finally called me and asked me to come get her. I came in and said, "Hey, do you wanna get out of this place?" "Yes!" she cried. "Okay, let's go!" I said, and away we went.

Once at my house, she asked for her checkbook, which she then stuffed into the front of her pants and announced, "I'm going to a hotel!" and took off up the street on foot. I found her lying on the grass in a neighbor's yard. She eventually fell asleep at home in a chair, and thankfully she woke the next morning without a mention of the day before. It was her moving day, and she was devastated to be leaving her friends (and boyfriend) in her community where she had lived for five years. She was 90 years old. She trusted me to find a good and safe place for her to live, and she was way more cooperative than I expected her to be as the spitfire lady she had always been. Losing her independence, her driver's license, and her autonomy was a huge blow, but it allowed us to spend more time together and to grow close as adults for the first time in our lives.

It was challenging, though, and for years I had been decreasing my work hours in order to have the time to give to Mom's increasing needs. Her many doctor appointments became excuses to go out to lunch. Picking up prescriptions became a reason to do more shopping, something she dearly loved. Mom loved nothing more than being turned loose in Costco with a shopping cart to steady her. I would keep a distant eye on her as she wandered up and down each and every aisle, tasting the samples and holding garments up to her to see if she liked them. Mom also loved being turned loose in JCPenney's. She could shop for dresses for hours!

When Mom needed so much that I, again and again, had to let go of teaching more classes in order to have the time she required, I felt resentment. How was I to maintain my sole source of income that way? But soon it occurred to me: What better thing could I possibly be doing with my time, my life, and my energy? So, I surrendered to it, leaning in and embracing my role. And it was hard. It was also fulfilling. It was an honor to be with her, be trusted by her, and to get to know her so intimately. And it was also heartbreaking. Seeing this woman, who had always wielded the sword of justice, reduced to someone who was completely dependent on others for everything, often reduced me to tears. I would leave Mom's foster care home, get into the car, and call my sister who had generously offered to be my sounding board. I would cry and sometimes wail, telling her everything that was happening. And I would walk with a friend that would listen and also share her mother's story.

Caring for Mom lovingly and helping her maintain some dignity was my goal. Knowing how important her appearance was to her, I would fix her hair, cut her nails, smooth rose-scented facial oil onto her thin, but still lovely, skin, and pluck the wiry hairs. Rubbing her hands and feet with lotion brought her comfort and human touch. Bringing her treats, and calling friends and family for her to talk to while I was there and could hold the phone for her, kept her connected. And listening to her stories was a joy. On hospice and medicated enough that she would not experience the terror of dementia nor any pain, she was able to enjoy the "visits" with her brothers and others who had long passed. She delighted in telling who she had seen, or sometimes was seeing. "Is that Lloyd over there? Who is that singing in the corner? Let's go to the party, shall we? Will you bring me a drink?" She told funny stories about wanting to dip meat in chocolate and that she was nursing not one, but two babies! Someone had brought them to visit and they were hungry, so she obliged them. My mom loved babies, and she was enjoying being useful again.

It was during this especially stressful time that I learned to ask for help. Mostly because I was desperate, but also because I had friends that had been through similar challenges with their mothers. One went with me to look at adult foster care homes, and went to visit with Mom so she wouldn't be alone when I had a cold and was not allowed to enter the hospital. Another friend's mother was in a foster home as well, and we started walking almost every day together, miles and miles, much farther than I would have ever gone on my own. And we talked. And she listened. And listened. And listened. I had other close friends that were my salvation as well. Friends that would ~again~ listen and listen and listen. They gave me hugs when I needed them. Took me on hikes and kayaking to get me out of my house and head. And they assured me that I was doing the right thing, the loving thing. And my family: my granddaughters, my niece and my nephew, and my older sister who came to give me moral support and to stay with Mom in the hospital and to help move her.

When Mom passed peacefully after eating breakfast one morning a few days before her 91st birthday, I was relieved. She had not suffered, nor had she lingered too long in her state of confusion. We'd had a wonderful visit the night before, and there were people coming to celebrate her upcoming birthday with her. The family still came, and we celebrated her with food and laughter and tears while going through family photos and reminiscing. The ordeal was over! Or so I thought. The worst was yet to come.

Mom's carefully crafted trust, with me as executor, put a target on my back. Those who didn't like what was happening blamed and attacked me. Family members began choosing sides and having rifts, and before I knew it, I had once close family members suddenly making my life very complicated. I was so confused. What was happening? Why were they being this way? Why weren't they HELPING me instead of FIGHTING me? A few were combative at first, and others just stopped talking to me, unfriended me on social media, or wouldn't take or return my calls or emails.

It was horribly distressing. I didn't understand any of it. I felt like I must be crazy. And then things got worse. One of my nephews died in a house fire, and a few days later, my dad had a stroke and died. Later that month, my dog died. I was a mess! I couldn't grieve when more losses kept happening. I began having anxiety attacks, and I was paralyzed with grief and fear. The family support was fractured and piecemeal. Yet I had legalities to attend to. There was one blessing in that my sister, who had lost her son, and I were reconciled after years of estrangement, united in the shared loss of our sons. I got it, and she could talk to me in ways unique to those who have suffered the loss of a child.

With the ongoing help of my good and patient friends, and the support of the family members ~ that were actually here and involved with my mother and who knew what she wanted and what I was trying to do ~ I was able to see the way forward. I called upon my mother, my grandmother, and my long line of strong women to guide and support me through the most difficult time of my life. The estate took years to settle, and I am still working to alleviate the recurring trauma around anything related to it and its administration.

I continue to seek out help from therapists, body workers, energy movers, and my friends and family who love and support me. I lean on my nephew and daughter-in-law, who call to check in and see how I am doing and express their love and loyalty. I have my grand-girls and great niece who visit regularly and whom I have the most gratitude for ~ they too, are becoming strong, courageous women. We still have fun, playing cards, going shopping and making art. I still have my dear friends who will listen and talk and walk miles and miles with me, who will sweep me away to the mountains or the shore, and who will give me a hug and tell me I am safe and whole. And I take a page from my ancestors, those strong women my young son was so aware of early on. I keep moving, keep laughing at every opportunity, keep showing up to support those I love in any and every way I can, and I keep loving my life, with all that it has brought and will bring.

Sit and rest a while
Take strength from your ancestors
Always here for you

~ Haiku on my family's memorial bench

ABOUT SANDI GOODWIN, MA, ERYT-500

Sandi Goodwin, MA, ERYT-500, Yoga and Meditation Teacher, Ayurvedic Health Counselor, and Posture Alignment Specialist.

Sandi loves all forms of self-expression and firmly believes in them as a tool for self-understanding and healing. A long-time practitioner and teacher of movement and mindfulness practices from dance and aerobics to Yoga, meditation, and embodiment, she really loves combining these with visual arts and writing for spiritual growth, and healing from grief and trauma through gathering in community.

Her degrees and certifications reflect her passion to grow and evolve through self-empowerment and spiritual evolution. A lifelong learner, Sandi loves to walk, hike, camp, travel, dance, create, and play with her special needs puppy. Long retired from 19 years of teaching public and private school education, and recently retired from 17 years of teaching yoga and meditation, Sandi is now focused on writing poetry, memoir, and young adult fiction. She is excited about being in her 60's, embracing silver hair, wisdom lines, and an abundant waistline as evidence of a fully lived life.

sandigoodwin@yahoo.com
www.mywordgarden.com

Chapter 5

SHE HAS RISEN: FLIGHT OF THE PHOENIX

Criselda Brooks, MS

"There's nothing stronger than a woman who has rebuilt herself."
– Hannah Gadsby

DENIAL

Even though he swore his threats were empty words, on this day, things went too far.

I still can't believe this is happening, I thought as I lay there looking out the second-floor window from my hospital bed. Despite all the disagreements we had, we were both hoping the relationship was fixable. When we woke up that morning, we didn't know this would be the day our relationship would go down in flames.

Despite the physical pain that I was in, my mind wanted to deny the fact that I was even in the hospital. I wished I were somewhere else. More than that, I wished this had never happened. If only I could rewind the tape. I kept thinking, *"This has to be a bad dream. I'll wake up any minute and laugh about how I thought it was real."* My fantasy was destroyed when a local sheriff slipped through the privacy curtain to take my statement and inquire about a protective order. Even though I knew I had to talk to him, I didn't want to. Just like I didn't want to tell the ambulance workers what happened. I'd probably have to repeat the story several times, but I didn't want to tell every doctor or nurse who walked into the room what had happened. I didn't want to even think about it because then I'd have to accept the truth that I'd been denying for so long.

The fact that I was in an abusive relationship became so visible that I could no longer ignore it. The day started very innocently. In fact, we had plans to go on a double date later that evening. I was working on my computer, eager to finish up for the day. Before I was done, he came in and asked, "Do you have something to tell me?" I felt accused by his tone of voice, and I'm sure my response wasn't gentle or soft.

Over the next 15 minutes, things escalated. Even though I normally didn't talk back or oppose him, I was unable to remain grounded. I yelled back. He pushed me. I lost my balance and stumbled. I scrambled to get back on my feet. He came towards me. I had nowhere to run. My back was literally against the wall when he punched me on my right side. Then, he turned around and left the room.

I crumbled to the floor and sat there, hugging my knees to my chest. In shock and pain, I didn't know what to do. My mind was spinning. *What just happened? Did he really just hit me? What do I do?* Still reeling, I reached for my phone to call the sheriff. When I tried to stand up, I screamed in pain and had to lower myself down onto the bed. Each subsequent inhale was suddenly more painful than the one before. At that point, my 19-year-old son heard me screaming and called 911. I was transported to the hospital in an ambulance. My partner was arrested. My son agreed to stay home to care for our pets. Without family or friends in the area, I had no one to call. I was alone.

By the time the sheriff was done with his questions, I couldn't help but feel like my life had been reduced to nothing more than a pile of ashes. All I could do was lie on the hard emergency room table, anxiously awaiting my test results. Even though I could feel the warmth of the morphine dancing through my veins, the pain was still unbearable. I tried to calm myself by taking deep breaths, but the fracture wouldn't allow my ribs to fully expand. When the head nurse came in to discuss my results, she calmly informed me that a liver laceration was causing internal bleeding. "I do need to inform you that if the bleeding doesn't stop on its own, we'll need to take you in for emergency surgery," she stated.

As soon as the words tumbled out of her mouth, I felt my heart drop and a wave of fear washing over me. In my mind, I was screaming, *No! This isn't happening! I will not need emergency surgery! If I make it, I refuse to have a horrible scar on my body to remind me of this day for the rest of my life!* If...I...make...it. "I know this is a lot, so I'll give you some time," she said politely before leaving the room.

Staring up at the ceiling, the nurse's words echoed in my mind. I suddenly realized ~ *I could die.* In that instant, my life flashed before my eyes. I went from being a curly-haired little girl clutching a rag doll to watching my son standing in his cap and gown. When the tear that rolled down my cheek splashed onto my hand, something changed. That tiny drop of water was like a bolt of lightning, igniting a fire within me that I didn't know I had. I wasn't ready to give up, but part of me felt helpless. *What can I do? How am I going to make it through this?* I asked myself. *I need a miracle.*

Then, I remembered the connection I'd been establishing with the Divine Feminine over the past four months. I'd only been an initiated priestess a few weeks, so even though I'd prayed to her before, those prayers were nothing compared to this. Still, I chose to believe in her glory, so I closed my eyes and said with conviction, "Thank you, Goddess, for stopping the bleeding and healing my body so I don't need surgery." When I surrendered and placed my trust in the Great Mother, the Divine Feminine energy I'd unknowingly stifled and suppressed my entire life began to awaken within me. It gave me a warm, fuzzy feeling inside. I knew it wasn't the morphine this time because I also felt a renewed sense of hope.

ANGER

Early that evening, I was admitted to the ICU. As the attendee maneuvered my wheeled bed down the long, empty corridors, I looked around in horror. *Isn't the ICU where the critical people go? Why are they taking me there? This must be really serious.* Apparently, I needed intensive care because the doctors weren't sure if the internal bleeding would stop on its own.

For someone usually too proud to ask for help, this was one of the most humbling experiences of my life. I had to swallow my pride and ask for help because I couldn't even use a bedpan on my own. Laying there listening to the incessant beeping of the machines, I started to feel angry. I was angry that I was in the hospital unable to even move on my own. I was angry at him for putting me in this situation and for all the times he'd made me miserable. Then, I was angry at myself for allowing him to treat me that way. *How did I not realize what was happening?*

There were red flags along the way. I'd worked in social services and had seen child abuse firsthand. Yet, I never saw the insults or name-calling directed at me as abusive. I suppose I'd been walking on eggshells for so long that it became normal to quietly accept his criticism, to keep the peace. Many times, I thought I deserved it. This changed when I was introduced to the Divine Feminine. I realized that I was worthy of happiness and that I deserved to be treated better. At that point, I began standing up for myself and refused to tolerate his abuse. However, this didn't make things better between us.

Once, he became so angry that he sprayed his 32 oz mug of hot coffee around the room. This resulted in permanent stains on the walls and ceiling. Another time, he punched my laptop and broke it, stating that I paid more attention to my work than to him. Unfortunately, I was too blinded by my rage, hurt, and resentment to own up to what the signs were telling me. Even my son warned me that things would get worse, but I was unable to accept what he was saying.

BARGAINING

The second day of my hospitalization, a physical therapist came in to see me. I was informed that I needed to start walking to keep blood clots from forming in my legs. In my mind, I screamed, *Leave me alone! I don't want to walk! I just want to curl up and feel sorry for myself. Can't you see I'm in pain?* Instead, I smiled and did the best I could to stand. Even though I was leaning heavily on the walker, the fracture made each step I took feel like I was being stabbed in the chest with a red-hot poker. Having to take short, shallow breaths, I was gasping for air after just one time around the nurses' station.

Throughout the day, various social workers and hospital staff came to chat. In their most professional manner, each one gently reminded me that if I remained in the same situation, next time could be worse. I knew they were right. If one hit at half force is all it took to break my ribs, I didn't want to imagine the damage his unleashed fury could create. They'd given me a lot to think about. When I was alone, I whispered to myself, "Great, what am I supposed to do now? Where do I go from here? If only..." Then, looking up to the Heavens I said, "Really? Isn't there something you can do to make this just go away? When is it my turn to be happy?"

Later that afternoon, a nurse informed me that my test results had improved enough for them to transfer me to a regular room. After a huge sigh of relief, I said, "Thank you, Goddess!" As the day turned into night, I did my best to clear my mind and quiet my racing thoughts. I didn't want to hear the constant chatter that made me wonder *what if*, so I forced myself to let it go and focus on my breathing. Unable to sleep, I started to think about where my life was headed. Unexpectedly, I heard a soft female voice in my head say, '*If you want things to be different this time, you have to find a way to forgive.*'

I knew that couldn't be one of my thoughts because forgiveness was the furthest thing from my mind. He'd ruined everything in a moment of unbridled anger, so why should I consider letting him off the hook? Then, I heard the voice again. It was louder this time. '*Whether you forgive or not, the choice is yours, and yours alone. Just think about what your life will be like if you don't.*'

DEPRESSION

Laying in a quiet hospital room alone gave me plenty of time to think. *Do I want to keep repeating the same mistakes I made in the past?* I asked myself. Even though I didn't lose my partner to death, I realized I was going through the stages of grief and loss. It made sense since I was losing someone who'd been in my life for many years. I was also losing a relationship and all the hopes and dreams that came with it. I'd already bounced back and forth between denial, anger, and bargaining. What I wanted most was to avoid the depression that's supposed to strike before acceptance sets in.

Even though I didn't know if I could find it in my heart to forgive (I'm a Scorpio, so forgiveness has never been by strong suit), something had to change. I knew what starting over in life looked like because I'd left an unhealthy marriage years earlier with nothing more than my 18-month-old son and whatever fit in the back-seat and trunk of my car. Whenever relationships didn't work out, I never stopped to consider why. I just blamed the guy and mended my broken wings because it was easier than finding fault with myself.

Here we go again, I thought. He'll go on his merry way living his life, while I'm here alone and miserable, becoming more cynical with each passing year. Huh, I guess hating him really isn't going to change anything for him now, is it? Then, it was like a light bulb came on and I had an Aha! moment. I suddenly realized that regardless of how much pain and rage I felt inside, it wouldn't affect him at all, but it would affect me. With this newfound insight, I knew that this could be my chance to truly start over. It could be my re-birth. My resurrection. Maybe I couldn't change what happened, but what if I could change the ending?

Or...

FORGIVENESS

Turning inward for answers, I began to grasp what the Great Mother was trying to teach me. She wanted me to realize that happiness and love weren't things to be found outside of myself. Everything I'd ever needed or longed for had always been inside of me, but I just didn't recognize it because it wasn't in the package I was expecting. The fears and judgments I carried weren't real ~ they were merely thoughts. By shifting my perspective from negative to positive, I could transform my reality. All it took was choosing the thoughts, words, and actions that aligned with the new life I wanted to create.

As I thought about what I should do, I couldn't help but picture myself on a dark, deserted highway standing at a railroad crossing with the ominous sound of an approaching train looming in the distance. I had to make a choice. If I chose the road of non-forgiveness, I could spend the rest of my life angry, resentful, and depressed. If I chose to take the road to forgiveness, maybe I could save myself some heartache or misery and have a chance at a happy life after all. At that moment, the choice was obvious. Forgiveness meant freedom; freedom from the fiery cage I'd built around myself, until I somehow found the strength to put the fire out.

I was allowed to go home on the third day. I felt better knowing he wouldn't be at the house because the emergency protective order had been approved. As glad as I was to be going home, I knew it would be difficult when I walked in the front door and was surrounded by his belongings. Every part of my being wanted to immediately start packing up his stuff and rearranging the house to my liking, but I physically couldn't. For the next 6-8 weeks, I'd be forced to slow down, work on my breathing, and focus on healing.

ACCEPTANCE

As soon as I felt well enough, I started working on creating my new life, starting with my house. At first, I wanted to be vindictive and make him pay for what he did. I thought about putting everything in trash bags by the curb or just destroying everything, but then I remembered my conversation with Goddess. She honored her part of the bargain by ensuring I didn't need surgery, so it was only fair to meet her halfway and try to exceed her expectations as well.

As I went through each room, I neatly boxed up his belongings. I folded his clothes and wrapped breakables in bubble wrap. Why? Because I also remembered that the divine would say "do unto others." I knew I'd appreciate receiving my things nicely packed if the situation was reversed, so that's what I did. At first, I thought, *This is a great way to show him that I'm not the horrible person he made me out to be.* By the time his friend picked up his belongings two months later, I realized that what he thought about me was irrelevant. I needed to show *myself* that I wasn't a horrible person because at the end of the day, *I* needed to like the person staring back at me in the mirror. More than that, I needed to love myself and establish a healthy relationship with myself.

When I finally embraced the slower pace I was forced to take, I started to see the world through a different lens. I continued to connect with the divine in ways I never knew possible. Eager to learn and heal emotionally, I started following the breadcrumbs Goddess sent me in various ways. I spent most of my time reading, studying and connecting. When I experienced a Kundalini awakening, I couldn't see the changes that were happening within, but I started to feel the energy around me shift. No longer feeling like my home was a danger zone, I was able to sink into the quiet depths of my soul undisturbed. One day, I realized what had changed. I wasn't overthinking and analyzing things to the point of anxiety anymore. The chatter was gone. For once, all was silent!

As I attuned myself to this new state, I was able to pay closer attention to my thoughts, feelings, and most importantly, my intuition. Before making decisions or acting on something, I started to pause and ask myself if I was about to come from a place of love or fear. I started to notice when something was causing a shift in my mood, so I was able to stop and analyze what I was feeling. I'd ask myself, *What is it about this situation that's causing me to feel this way?* I'd continue to ask myself questions until I figured out why it was bothering me. Once I figured out when the emotion started and why, I was able to reframe my thinking and see the situation in a new light.

As I got better at catching and releasing negative thoughts before they turned into emotions, I started to notice that I was reacting less to things in my daily life. When something happened that would normally upset me, it didn't bother me in the same way as before. I stopped becoming angry and frustrated when things didn't go my way. Instead, I found myself looking at the situation at hand from a place of compassion. So, instead of labeling something as "good" or "bad," I chose to see it as "something that happened." This allowed me to forgive others in my life for the "wrongs" I believed they committed against me. In doing so, I was also able to forgive myself for taking things personally when I shouldn't have, and for choosing not to let things go when I should have.

I started to see the world, and life, in a way I'd never experienced before. When I literally stopped to smell the roses one day, I didn't see the rose; I saw the beauty of its creation. Then, going deeper, I saw the mathematical sequence that tells each petal where to go. Everywhere I looked, I saw the same beautiful patterns of creation around me, and I finally understood the true meaning of "we are one."

Caught up in these moments of awe on an almost daily basis, I went from feeling content to being in a state of peace and perfect bliss. I felt like I'd found Heaven on Earth. I felt connected to nature, the universe, the divine, and everyone around me. I felt as large and expansive as the universe and as small as an atom at the same time. I was everything and nothing. In those moments of connectedness, I cried for humanity and all those suffering in the world. Then, for the first time since the incident, I cried as I forgave myself for the mistakes I made in the past and the lessons I'd refused to learn. As I gently wiped the tears from my eyes, the love and light emanating from Goddess enveloped me like a mother holding her child.

I'll always remember that this new chapter in my life started with finding my worth and the courage to leave an unhealthy relationship. Forgiveness was just one of the many lessons along the way waiting to be discovered. Now that I've accepted the Divine Feminine, and have found inner peace, I'm ready to rise like a Phoenix from the ashes of my shattered dreams, spread my wings, and fly!

About Criselda Brooks, MS

Criselda Brooks, MS aspires to be a beacon of hope. As an initiated priestess and certified astrology practitioner, Criselda blends her commitment to personal growth with the spiritual elements of the Divine Feminine. She holds a Master's Degree in Sociology and dedicated ten years to the field of social services.

While working with children in a therapeutic foster care setting, she had the honor of helping many be adopted into their forever homes. She also trained and supervised court appointed volunteers who advocate in family court for the children's best interests.

Criselda currently resides in Central Texas with her son and a spirited Yorkie. When she's not busy running her landscaping business, she can be found reading, writing, or playing the saxophone.

Email address: **author@criseldabrooks.com**
Website: **www.CriseldaBrooks.com**

Criselda's gift to you:
"The Empowered Woman Within: Unlock Your Potential."

Visit: **criseldabrooks.com/free-workbook** for your free copy.

Chapter 6

A Walk in the Field of Courage
Planting Seeds of Courage & Change

Jennifer Andrews, MA

*Courage is a guiding light,
even when shadows of despair threaten to consume us.
~ Jennifer Andrews*

If I can only be better. If I can only do everything right. If I can be perfect for my family... if I can be good enough ~ then maybe I can fix what feels so wrong. These were the thoughts of my 14-year-old self as I hefted the weight of the gun, heavy in my hand. The long, steel barrel was cold. I remember the bullets feeling so solid, so powerful, and they made a clinking sound when I rolled them around and through my fingers. I placed the bullets on the bedspread and picked up the .357 Magnum that was kept in my parents' bedroom for home security. I wasn't sure how to load it, so I began to explore the gun more fully. I pulled the hammer back and then pulled the trigger. The hard snap and POP of pulling the trigger of this unloaded gun will forever be etched in my mind.

Once I discover how this weapon gets loaded and how I would shoot it, I will have a decision to make. Will I, or won't I, commit suicide? As I sat thinking about and seeing the aftermath of what I would leave my family, my Soul screamed a loud, clear, and strong "NO!" The vision of blood splattered onto the walls, the pool of blood that would soak into their bed, and the body of their second born daughter lying dead with a fatal gunshot wound to the head was more than my consciousness could bear.

With trembling hands, tears running down my face, and my heart beating faster than I had ever known possible, I replaced the gun and bullets right where they had been stored. I closed the closet door and then sat for a very long time on the edge of their bed, full of fear, doubt and shame. Strangely enough, I had some level of awareness that it had been an act of courage not to commit suicide. The longer I sat on the bed, I knew that I would have to also find the courage to speak the truth to my parents about how I had almost taken my own life that afternoon. That very night I did somehow find the courage to tell my parents the depths of my despair, and I asked them for help. This is how I first ended up in therapy at age 14.

Looking back, that moment with the gun was not isolated – it was the culmination of years of inner turmoil. In my attempt to unconsciously navigate my intense childhood emotions, I developed coping mechanisms rooted in perfectionism. Thoughts like these shaped and influenced my behaviors of always doing the right thing, or being good enough, as a child and adolescent. On that afternoon, I felt as if there was no hope and that everything was my fault because I wasn't "good enough," so I almost took my life.

Before this unforgettable afternoon, I had been caught in a relentless dance with intense feelings of confusion, abandonment, fear and uncertainty. I knew I was loved by my dad, my mom and my older sister, but I felt incredibly lost and alone in life. No, this first exposure to therapy wouldn't fix everything, but it did lay to rest the one and only time I considered suicide in my life.

Tending the Garden

My first experience in therapy planted seeds that would take years to blossom, ultimately shaping my education and my career path. It was as if that one courageous step at 14 had unknowingly set me on a trajectory of self-discovery and service. After high school I pursued undergraduate and master's degrees in psychology. I completed various internships and countless hours of supervision. I passed a licensing exam. I became a Marriage and Family Therapist to help others the way I had been helped.

The truth is that despite years of preparation and a deep desire to help others, I found myself disillusioned not long after becoming a Marriage and Family Therapist. I simply did not love what I was doing as a therapist the way I had anticipated. Yes, I had my office, I had a schedule book with the names of my clients dispersed here and there. I had a sign on the door, and I was "doing the thing I was supposed to be doing because this is what I set out to do." I should have been happy and excited to show up every day to help others and to be their therapist. I wasn't. What I thought would be my life's calling, to be a therapist serving others, began to feel misaligned, and I knew I was in deep trouble when I no longer wanted to unlock my office door. It had nothing to do with my clients. I knew the proper therapeutic techniques to help them, my schedule book was full, and amongst my colleagues I was referred to as a "very good" and "sound" therapist. No, the fact that I didn't want to unlock my office door had everything to do with me.

The discomfort inside me was impossible to ignore. Instead of satisfaction and joy, I was feeling unhappiness, discord, and discontentment. I deeply questioned how these emotions could be washing through me after all the time I had spent, and all my hard work to become a well-respected therapist. For a long period of time, I just thought it was something that I needed to work through. I believed it was something that would pass, or that I would get over. However, I wasn't getting over anything. The only thing that was happening was that my discontent, dis-ease, and unhappiness was growing stronger. Then, I started to add shame and fear to the list of emotions moving within me. I was ashamed to admit my internal state of affairs to anyone. I was simply afraid of what I was feeling. Of course, this was not in the best interest of, or in service to myself or my clients.

The dance between the intense emotion of fear and courage is what I would have to learn to navigate. I was so afraid that by acting upon any of this, I would be making the wrong choices and that I would be irresponsible. Yes, I was also terrified that I was going to disappoint people if I admitted my true feelings. To further the anguish, I then took into consideration that I wouldn't make enough money for my family if I wasn't a therapist, and the cherry on the top ~ I would be looked down upon by everyone if I no longer wanted to be a therapist. There were so many reasons to just remain here, playing the role of a therapist, for the rest of my career.

Simultaneously, deep inside of me I knew that all those reasons were being imposed upon me from outside ideals and percep-tions. To be courageous at this juncture of my life, I had to feel and listen inside to what my truths were and are. I had to be will-ing to continually listen, change, and to evolve.

A TIME FOR GROWTH

Many years later, life led me to another profound moment of change. On a crisp Autumn evening, I walked into the yoga studio that had become my sanctuary. This was the studio where for years I had been studying yoga and meditation for my own growth and solace. I even completed my own yoga teacher training program for the sole purpose of my personal growth...

or so I thought. I had taken this familiar short trek from my car to the studio door so many times before.

However, this evening, I stopped so that I could take notice of how the Autumn leaves instinctually released themselves from the trees they had securely held onto throughout Spring and Summer. The leaves danced in the air as they surrendered to gravity and fell to the Earth. I could deeply sense Fall was in the air, a sign that change was coming.

I walked into the studio and found an open spot in the circle of women attending the meditation workshop. The overhead lights were dim. There was a beautiful bouquet of flowers to one side of the teacher, and a dramatic flickering flame of a candle to the other. This woman, who was radiant, poised and elegant, would one day become one of the most influential females in my life. This was the night I met my meditation teacher.

Under her beautifully skilled guidance, we workshop attendees embarked on a weekend meditation adventure. By the time it came to completion, something profound had awakened within me. The evocative meditation workshop stirred whispers deep in my Soul, and these whispers were beckoning to be heard. Years later, I would courageously follow these whispers to a new life, leaving behind the profession of Marriage and Family Therapy to become a yoga and meditation teacher, a yoga studio owner and a world-wide retreat leader and presenter.

That night changed everything for me. Watching the leaves release their grip on the branches, swirling through the air before settling gently on the Earth, carried a meaning I hadn't fully understood at the time. Later in life, I too would let go, releasing my license as a Marriage and Family Therapist, to land where I was truly meant to be. This surrender led me to the path my Soul had always intended: guiding others as a teacher and mentor through yoga and meditation.

Ultimately, changing the course of my life was by no means easy. Big changes in life often come with layers of complexity, and particulars that will require a lot of navigation. Changing the course of your life might take years, as it did for me. It will require the courage and the willingness to listen to all the communication from your Soul; sometimes it is a whisper, and sometimes a loud and powerful shout. Nothing can be rushed; it all must unfold in due time.

TIME TO BLOOM

So, once again, and for the second time in my life, I found myself in need of a therapist. Over twenty-five years after my first experience in therapy, I sought out help. The struggles I faced now felt eerily similar to those I had encountered in my youth and adolescence, though this time, they stemmed from a crisis of purpose rather than survival.

I stepped through the threshold for my initial session with my new therapist and made my way to her lovely and comfortable couch. As I took a seat, memories of my first experience in therapy came flooding back. The feelings of needing help from someone outside of myself were real and unsettling. This time, however, I felt as if I should be able to figure this out on my own, but the fact was, I couldn't find any true resolve for how I was feeling inside.

As she asked me the standard 'initial session' questions, I had such appreciation for what my own clients must feel when they step through my door. I looked around her tidy and inviting therapy room, taking in the color on the walls and her chosen décor. I noticed where the tissue box was located, what degrees hung behind her, and how many books she had on the bookshelf. I made my comparisons between her office and mine and I politely answered her questions as we made our way through this initial session. She knew I was also a therapist, so we could talk on a different level about why I was here to see her.

Through my answers, the picture I painted for her was one of being happily married with children at home, a career on the rise, and a palpable amount of discontent and dis-ease within myself. As I gave voice to my current and presenting issues, it was obvious to both of us that the insidious energy of perfectionism was what was coursing through my veins.

The toxicity of perfectionism within the purpose of my own life's work had gotten the better of me, and I was losing the battle once again. Under the influence of perfectionism, I feel like I am either too much or not enough, I am either too smart or too dumb, too fat or too thin, too pretty or not pretty enough, too young or too old, too this or too that, too good or not good enough.

Ultimately it always ends up that I'm not good enough, and once again I was losing the battle with these debilitating energies known as perfectionism. To the credit of my first therapist, she never truly addressed this with me at age 14. There just were not enough sessions for that kind of therapy. No, for the limited number of sessions that had been approved by the insurance company, her target was my contemplation with suicide. She did a magnificent job in that department, because thoughts of suicide have never been back on my radar screen. However, what was missed all those years ago was the deeper, underlying reasons as to why I felt so lost and alone.

Now, years later, as I sat on the therapy couch for the second time in my life, I realized that I was still living through the veil of "not being good enough." The trigger this time was not family oriented. No, this time the trigger was how I was truly feeling about my career. What I chose not to put into the picture I painted for my new therapist in that first session was the truth about not wanting to be a therapist anymore. I am not entirely sure why I made the conscious choice not to say anything to her about that key point, but I can tell you it had something to do with me lacking the courage to speak the truth to anyone outside of myself.

At the end of our first session, she mapped out her plan. As sincere as she was, her plan felt too canned and ordinarily prescribed. Following typical protocol, she would submit to my insurance company the need for multiple sessions, and then she left me with a beacon of hope. Her hope was that by the end of our work and time together, things would be much better in my life.

I graciously smiled and thanked her for her time. She had conducted a very sound initial session with me, and I was grateful. As I walked away from her office and realized that she was not able to elicit my truth, I knew I would never return. I needed to be somewhere where I could courageously claim my truth and meditation was that place. Suddenly, I began to feel deeply grateful for the profound realization that therapy was not what I needed, for this was something only I could uncover within myself.

Stepping over the threshold of that door to exit meant I was stepping into a field of courage. A profound and deep shift occurred within me as I left her office that day. My years of devotion to yoga and meditation began to fully blossom, bear fruit, and guide me. Daily practices became non-negotiable and continue to be so to this day. From this single session, I had a revelation of how to heal myself on my own terms. I felt the embrace of my own divine Soul wisdom, and it was time to deeply heal.

Simultaneously, I realized "Wow, I think I am meant to work with others through the teachings of yoga and meditation, and not as a therapist." As this realization came into greater clarity, so did apprehension about not being a therapist in the world. I wasn't interested in making a rash decision, but I could no longer deny the truth that my life needed profound change. I could no longer deny the true call of my purpose.

So, I have stuck to my resolve of helping others. However, I have left the Western approaches which had felt too prescribed, too limiting, and too cookie-cutter. I have fully embraced the more freeing Eastern approaches and practices of yoga and meditation. This is what is mine to offer the world, and how I choose to guide and help others.

Reaping What Was Sowed

Most of the time my divine Soul communicates with me through sweet whispers that feel like they are steeped in benevolence and serenity. There have been a few occasions that I have received communication as a stern, loud voice. The loud voice is also loving and still permeated with benevolence, but this voice is undeniably strong, firm and confident. No matter what voice I hear from my divine Soul, I have learned to never ignore her communication. Her voice, the voice of deep feminine wisdom, is always to be revered.

So, the decision was made, and I embraced my daily meditation practices with all my heart. It was there, in the quiet of inner reflection, that I was able to hear the whispers: It is time. With true inner courage and trust I was able to answer in return, YES, it is time. From that point forward, I didn't look back. My focus shifted entirely to deepening my relationship with my divine Soul. Letting go of the need for external validation, I courageously told my colleagues I would be leaving the profession. Some understood, and most did not.

Regardless, I removed my name from the office door, packed up my belongings, closed the door, and locked it by turning the key one final time. Hence, I closed that chapter of my life. I surrendered my therapist license, relinquishing the professional identity that had once defined me. In doing so, I began walking on a new path ~ one rooted in authenticity and guided by my true calling.

Vulnerability and strength marked each step, and as I listened to my Soul, my passion for working with others as a yoga and meditation teacher flourished. Undeniably, each step of the journey has held meaning and purpose, revealing that life itself is a process of evolution and growth ~ for me, and for you. Stepping fully into my true Soul path required immense courage, but it is a decision I will never regret.

The foundation for this transformation was built on years of studying yoga and meditation, alongside the knowledge and skills I cultivated as a therapist. Though I no longer can call myself a therapist (I gave up that right when I surrendered my license), my time spent as a formal therapist continues to shape how I mentor and teach. Decades of education, devotion, and personal growth have woven themselves into my approach, offering a depth that is unmistakably my own.

As I align with my Soul essence, I feel the radiance of doing what I was designed to do. This alignment is not just an inner knowing but is affirmed in the outer world. Opening my studio called Yoga Sol, co-creating a yoga school, and leading teacher training programs were just the beginning. I've joyfully developed meditation courses for women and co-led retreats around the globe. Invitations to share my teachings at international Women's Conferences further affirm that I am walking the path meant for me.

Everything I do is infused with love, integrity, joy, grace, and ease. This journey is not about being better than anyone else. It is about becoming the best version of myself. Vulnerability, strength, and courage have been my steadfast companions since childhood, guiding me through every hurdle and misstep. What once felt like insurmountable mistakes, barriers or challenges, now appear as necessary parts of the journey. The perfectionism that once coursed through my veins has been replaced by self-compassion and love, healed through my inner practices. Meditation and yoga have brought immeasurable gifts into my life ~ gifts I believe are available to you as well.

I have such compassion for anyone who has contemplated suicide. I, myself, stepped very close to that edge, and then courageously stepped back into the full embrace of life. I also have immense respect for anyone that decides to change the course of their life so that they can walk on the path their Soul has put in front of them. When the shadows of despair almost consume us, trust that we can be guided by the shimmering light of courage.

So, may we all find the courage to listen to the truth of our Souls. May we honor the calls that arise within us again and again. May we all Walk in The Field of Courage.

ABOUT JENNIFER ANDREWS, MA

Jennifer Andrews, MA, holds a master's degree in clinical psychology and lives in Carson City, Nevada, with her husband. She has three adult children, and three dogs, all of whom she loves and adores. She has been studying and teaching yoga and meditation for over 25 years. She supports women ages 40–85 joyfully guiding them toward their Soul path of living with Grace, Wholeness, Ease, and Purpose.

Jennifer is the founder of Yoga Sol, co-founder of the Bhavana School of Yoga, and a board member of The Radiance Sutras Institute. She leads teacher trainings, international retreats, and meditation immersion programs, specializing in Meditation Secrets for Women and Instinctive Meditation. Jennifer's teaching style is comprehensive, nurturing, fun-loving, and supportive, offering practices that honor each individual's unique path.

Jennifer Andrews, MA
Website: **www.jennandrews.com**
Email: **jenn@jennandrews.com**

Chapter 7

COURAGE, COMPASSION AND LOVE: MY JOURNEY WITH MARY MAGDALENE

Melanie Ann Baron

COURAGE

When I stepped into more detailed preparation for our book, all my plans and concepts for this chapter changed in a second. In a shamanic journey, the mountain lion, power animal of my solar plexus chakra, appeared as a guide. In fact, it was a female. She positioned herself in front of me, impressive in her power, and stared at me. Bright light glistened in the amber of her eyes. Whether it came from the sun, or radiated from inside of her, I couldn't tell, but it was so intense, so irresistible, that it completely caught my attention.

"It's all about courage," she said unexpectedly, trying to cover a hidden smile playing across her noble face. She repeated: *"It's all about courage,"* looking at me with her sparkling eyes.

"Remember..."

On my inner screen she started to show me pictures leading into my journey beginning in January 2020. Covid ruled over the lands. I had just arrived from paradise, from beautiful Hawaii, straight into the German winter.

Immediately, I was forced to move into a new flat, just a few days before the lockdown started. I found myself stranded in a small place, surrounded by boxes of stuff from a former life. It seemed surreal. I nearly drowned in an ocean of unsorted things. Being alone and cut off from the world around me played heavily on the shadows of my childhood memories, and awakened states of helplessness, sadness and despair. I had to find a way to get on without the practical help of others. Giving up was not an option.

I decided to create an island of rest, peace and harmony in the middle of these stormy waves that raged inside and outside. I needed a shelter, a safe place, a sacred ground. With all my love, I built an altar, beautiful and radiant. All of a sudden, I was not alone anymore. The masters, goddesses and angels now became my company, my guides, and my guardians in uncertain times.

As a next step I found an online course about success in life. Pretty ironic in the actual field of existence I had created. As I eagerly followed the daily modules over a period of 33 days, including physical exercises and meditations, I was able to hold a structure and purpose for this bizarre period of time. I was meditating, dancing, listening, reflecting, and journaling. I tried to fill most of my day with meaningful activities of high vibration. Slowly settling down, I surrendered to the presence, here and now. I call it "Surrender to the Gods," when nothing helps and no solution seems to rise at the horizon.

All that is left to do is to stop thinking, stop wanting and stop planning. Leave space for God to act. Let the Universe take over, because whatever you figure out in your clever mind will be just a smaller picture of the true potential you hold. Let go. Hand it over. *Trust*, I told myself repeatedly, like a mantra, everything will be fine. It takes more courage to let go of control than to constantly hold a hard grip of all the threads.

The intense process of this online project evolved as proper shadow work. As usual, when your higher guides speak to you, it is not about small issues. Ask and you will be given. Don't expect it to be what you thought, what you wanted, or what seems cozy and comfortable for you. The Universe delivers. It challenges you, and it always wants you to step up, leap out of your comfort zone and dare to bravely walk the path of your Higher Self. Full commitment: no compromises, no shortcuts, no excuses. Remember, YOU were the one asking and YOU were the one figuring out this experience long before you incarnated on this planet. Courage is needed more than anything else. Just walk and trust.

"*Write a book!*" was the answer I received in one of the courses meditations. *Seriously, are you kidding?* my brain responded sarcastically and slightly amused. It turned out to be the next phase of my life ~ my personal road of success and happiness. The result of this inner journey was neither another workshop, nor a relationship, nor a healing treatment, but a book. In crystal-clear bright colors, I was shown how I stood in a bookshop, signing my book in a presentation, smiling and beaming in joy. I needed to breathe. And yes, I was wearing a red dress ~ an important detail.

My higher management hadn't finished creating a spiritual business plan yet. My guides were getting into detail: telling me the exact title, the structure, the number of chapters, subtitles, each picture, plus the whole layout of the book inside and outside. I was speechless and completely overwhelmed. That was nothing like I had expected. Yes, sure, I had some ideas about concepts for a book in the back drawers of my mind, but this went far beyond everything I ever imagined. I'd often thought about writing a book. My life has been full of adventures, magical moments, little miracles even. But spirit gave me another topic that was more important, more urgent, and more challenging. It had to contain 13 chapters with a very sacred title. It had to be channeled, reporting moments when I received transmissions, visions, and revelations.

So after all, it was time to present myself as a channel medium. I had to write about masters and about spiritual truth. Seeing my name written on the cover of a channeled book called, *"The Golden Book of Love,"* gave me goosebumps. It was a mix of total bliss and fear at the same time.

Then came day 13, this magical day in my online training, when everybody was supposed to start the practical implementation, which meant writing the first page of my book. Collectively we inaugurated a little ceremony: I lit a candle, burned some palo santo, prepared my favorite music and opened a new empty document on my laptop. My heart pumped and my pulse must have doubled, it was so exciting....

Surprisingly, I had underestimated the valuable clues my guides had given me. It was so much easier than I had thought. I just simply started to write, as if I had never done anything else. The words poured out of my fingers, filling the document like a wave of light covering the page. It was easy, there was no effort required, spirit seemed to let me have a powerful dictation. The inner screen that my lioness friend had switched on seemed to shift to the next level of this cosmic game.

Courage suddenly needed to develop in another file of my consciousness. Unexpectedly, it came along with fear, with shivers crawling up my neck and doubts, interrupting the natural flow of this sacred wave of writing. Disturbing phantoms started to raise and whisper into my ears, occupied my thoughts and created fog in my brain. Dark clouds appeared like a storm over my sunny ocean. *"What are you doing here? What are you writing? What about the reactions of people reading it? Who are you to write about Jesus, about Mary Magdalene, about spiritual entities and sacred wisdom?"*

But there was this other voice too, the higher voice, the voice of my soul. It persisted, staying with me, talking to me, repeating over and over again: "*You're ok, you're doing fine. Keep going, you can do it.*" I felt supported, guided and loved like never before. It felt so right, so *me*... as if my whole life had been preparing me for nothing but that.

The more I wrote, the content became more courageous, more daring. I observed myself creating words of deep truth, so meaningful that I couldn't believe it was really me writing. I experienced my courage and will, the joy and the love inside being bigger than any fear, doubt, or argument of my critical brain. I felt so powerful fulfilling that task. Exploring a part of myself which must have been hidden somewhere in a fold of my soul, somewhere in the chests of my past lives, somewhere written in the stars. This is part of my mission. I just knew it. I felt it, and it made me smile. It made me happy. It nurtured me.

Courage occurred in other disguises. It also showed up as encouragement for the readers. The chapters created a certain mosaic and intertwined to a very unique journey. Each chapter guides into one facet of love and courage, like a gem hidden inside. Reading a rebellious book, naming issues which might provoke or even offend others, adds to it. A book different from most of the mainstream content is not always obvious.

I became aware of my own courage to step into that adventure, the courage which is needed to stand for every word I was guided to write, to sign it with my name and find myself in public probably sharing those words with an unknown crowd.

And most of all, how much courage must have been required by the protagonists in their lives, at their time. How much unbreakable courage Jesus must have had to maintain. How infinitely brave Mary Magdalene must have been to spread her truth in this very traditional and hostile male world that surrounded her:

a world threatening her and her beloved ones, dangerous for those who followed. A world in which they risked their lives, and not just a few of them were killed.

Is that ancient fear still running in our blood, sitting in our bones, right in the marrow? Is this why women of our times need even more courage to share their truth?

What a clever move of my guardian lioness to raise all these aspects just in time to write this chapter. While my own book is growing steadily.

Beside the unexpected support of my feline guide, the presence of Mary Magdalene's spirit at my side was a main factor, helping me to carry on. She was my pillar to be strong. In 2017, she appeared in my life sharing her own story. She became my role model and beloved teacher. Our first encounter was magic and changed my whole personal path of evolution and destiny.

COMPASSION

My trip to the South of France in summer 2017 was a long-cherished dream of mine, my deepest desire at that time. I was ready to answer the call of my heart, to listen to my intuition and follow the traces of Mary Magdalene's life in Europe. I planned to visit the famous places in Provence mentioned in numerous sources connected to her possible legacy. Every cell was burning to experience and explore them myself with all my senses.

I hadn't visited this region for many years, but it was clearly imprinted in my dreams and fond memories of my early twenties. After a long break, I had the chance to return to Provence. There are no coincidences.

Every time I inhale the scent of lavender and let my gaze wander over the typical hilly landscape, my soul seems to breathe a sigh of relief. The magic of Southern France, its plants and animals and the typical vivid mentality of the people had cast a colorful spell on me. The sunlight making the air shimmer is unique and famous among painters worldwide. It conjures up a glittering veil, a prism of light over every tree, every house, everything, allowing the eye to relax and just glide. It feels like my soul essence; my deepest core is happy in these special moments of divine.

I didn't know why at the time, but I had a kind of premonition that I had found another magic fractal of the mosaic of my life, which was waiting to be discovered and unveiled.

On the second morning of my journey, however, everything was different. I sat alone in the silent area for prayers and meditation in front of the altar of the Basilica in Saint-Maximin-la-Sainte-Baume, a tiny town northeast of Marseille. This church, dedicated to Mary Magdalene, is very unique. According to tradition, she lived in this area for many years in the second half of her life and ascended here. Her relics are protected in a chest, guarded in the crypt of the church and her skull is kept visible in a glass shrine surrounded by a shiny golden frame.

I was not centered and felt sad and hurt after a heavy argument with my travelling companion. Longing to be alone, I took time to meditate and reflect, to recover my energy and sort out where I was in that emotional drama. I contemplated in my prayers and sunk into the calm atmosphere to finally enjoy peace.

Suddenly a soft presence occurred ~ strong and yet subtle. Although I could neither comprehend nor believe what happened, I could not deny that a soft energy of translucent light seemed to appear right next to me. I hardly dared to breathe. As if she was suddenly sitting beside me on the pew, I felt her gentle vibration all over me. It was different than usual. She was not above me in my vertical channel of energy as I know it from many years being a channel medium of ascended masters and angels. This time she was almost physically present, tangible, just there, like a familiar person, a friend to my right, sitting there beside me. A light fragrance of roses surrounded us and it seemed like a blissful dream, a sweet meditation, a state of trance.

A warm shower of energy ran through my body, an unknown quiet joy and love filled me from inside, and tears ran down my cheeks in that magical moment. I heard her soothing voice, and like a mother, speaking to her beloved child, she whispered in my right ear, insistently and with infinite love:

"Beloved one, Dear, it is me...

You know me; to find me you have come to this place.
I am Mary of Magdala, the companion of Jesus.
The one you have been looking for, for so long. It is me.

This church is my temple, here is my Spirit. Here is my Essence.
Do not search any longer, I am here. My Essence is free. This is where my Spirit dwells, in sacred places like this.

Follow your heart, I will guide you, you are at the right place at the right time.

Trust me, I am with you, I will be at your side from now on.

Listen to me, here and now. It is important for you to understand.
Now is the moment when your soul is foreseen for the next step, when you will walk through the doors of revelation.

*Now you are ready and now you allow to receive.
This is what I wish to share:*

And if they are in anger with you, be love.

And if they offend you, love them and forgive.

And if they do not understand, be patient and bless them.

And if they ridicule and expose you, capture the fear that leads them astray, the uncertainty, the despair and hold them in your soft arms of safety.

And if they don't fulfill what you have expected, don't wait, be the love that redeems the lack.

And whenever they cause you pain, feel the pain that torments their soul and pray for them.

And when they shout at you, take their words into your divine vessel of transformation, understand the cries of their hearts and transform them into the sacred balm of healing.

And when tears well up in your eyes, feel the grief that rises within you, let them become tears of compassion, tears of mercy, that save the child within you from drowning."

Her powerful key message echoed in my mind, like an eternal prayer, and she continued talking to me:

> "As the words of my beloved Yeshua taught us, love does not mean giving, bound by conditions and favorable fates, never dependent on the love, the words, or the behavior of others. Love does not judge, never.

You think you are not able to do that, my love?

You think that it would be too much to ask, too difficult, too unfair and one-sided, after everything that just happened to you? After all, you think that has been done to you?

Be aware that I was persecuted, betrayed, ridiculed. I was humiliated, punished, banned and hurt. No one showed respect, except for a few gentle souls following me.

Do you really think it was easy?

Do you really think my life on Earth was easier than yours?

MY BELOVED, BELIEVE ME...
IF I COULD DO IT, SO CAN YOU. TRUST...

I am at your side, never forget!"

LOVE

Fulfilled and deeply touched, I left the Basilica. My heart leapt with excitement, feeling how coherently her words resonated in me. My brain was confused, desperate, my ego full of fear of failing and not being able to meet these demands. Sure, I had known it for a long time, had read about it in many books, lived it and practiced unconditional love. Knowing it doesn't mean you have to live it to the fullest in all domains of your life.

Her advice struck me: I realized how often I still acted against my better knowledge, against my inner voice, against my divine guidance, my Higher Self. Many times I still lost myself in the effort to fulfill the needs of others instead of listening within and trusting my heart. I wasted my energy pointlessly and followed the critical commandments and judgments of my childhood, blindly walking into the traps of ego and my drama of not being 'good enough'.

Walking back from the church, my Higher Self, initiated an inner dialogue, a kind of personal deep talk with the wisdom of my soul. Grasping the more subtle levels of unconditional love in its immaculate purity led me to the mysterious path of compassion and mercy. Both are long-forgotten, often disregarded qualities, without which it is hardly possible to escape the deceptions and illusions of life and to feel the essence of love and compassion.

Love is a state of being within you, nourished by the divine source, created, sustained and infinitely flowing, by the loving heart of Father/Mother God. Compassion for yourself and others is the first step. It forms the bridge to unconditional love.

Mercy and forgiveness are the second steps. They challenge you, demand more from you, penetrating deeper into the wounds of the heart that are barely healed from the battles you fought. Guilt no longer exists, not as an excuse, not as a defense, and not as a reason to distract from your own injuries.

Compassion knows no hierarchy, no being right, no competition, no wanting to win. Compassion is an eternal state of flow in permanent communion with the Divine Source.

"Ephphatha," said Yeshua in the Gospel of Mark (Chapter 7, 31-37).

In Aramaic it means "Open up!". Those were the only words he used and the deaf-mute was healed. Compassion and love in deep unity with the Divine was the only vibration in his heart. Everything else had lost its meaning.

Open yourself to love, because it is always there. It is beyond every limitation of your mind, your emotions, or your experiences.

Melanie Ann Baron

Open yourself to love, unconditionally, because it holds you, nourishes you, carries you, strengthens you, and saves you.

It is not on the outside, as it may seem. It is the light within yourself, the energy from which you are created, and the building block for the origin of this universe. It is the primordial molecule from the beginning of life, the foundation stone of creation. It is the multiversal glue that holds together everything that exists. From the stones, plants, animals and people to the stars, the planets, the galaxies, the cosmos, and the universes.

Love is the particle, the bioplasm that forms the nothingness between all that is. Love is the all-encompassing and everlasting abundance inside the vacuum of creation. Love IS.

Seven years later, completing this chapter, Mary Magdalene proclaimed in my morning meditation:

> *"To all you wonderful women, healers, wise women, brave women, lightworkers and teachers, I have come to guide you into a new world. I have reached out to many of you spreading the message of love and truth. Now you are needed, now your words will be heard, you chose to be here. Your light is the torch in dark times, your wisdom is the red thread to find the way out of the maze of confusion. Your experience is the sacred tool to lead humankind into a radiant future. It has been previewed thousands of years before.*
>
> *This is the moment when consciousness rises and evolution takes place. We are all here to bring love. I am at your side. May peace prevail on Earth."*

~ Melanie Ann Baron
December 2024

About Melanie Ann Baron, Yllari Saaskun, MSeD

Melanie Ann Baron, YLLARI SAASKUN, is a spiritual teacher, coach, channel medium and healer in Germany.

For over 30 years, she has shared her wisdom and expertise in the fields of shamanic healing, lightwork and meditation, following the path of her Higher Self.

Melanie studied alternative healing methods of the women's health movement and worked alongside indigenous elders and wisdom keepers in Hawaii, Peru, Mexico and Europe.

She has received initiations at sacred places worldwide. Her passion is to guide people on spiritual pilgrimages to discover the power spots of Mother Earth and find the message of their soul.

Since 2016 she has dedicated her work to spreading the wisdom of the Sacred Feminine. Inspired by Mary Magdalene's transmissions, she writes, gives conferences, and leads trainings and events to initiate women into the qualities of the Goddess.

Her mission is to support humankind in a new consciousness of love and compassion during these evolutionary times.

Melanie's spiritual name, YLLARI SAASKUN, is a fusion of Quechua and Mayan, and means 'From the dawn into the light' ~ the motto of her life.

Please send me an email, or DM me on Instagram or Facebook to get your free gift!

Linktree: **https://linktr.ee/info.i.m.baron**
Email: **info@melanieannbaron.com**

Chapter 8

HOW I MET GOD THE MOTHER

Shuna Morelli MS, LMT, CH

*"For thousands of years,
a deeply wounded masculine energy
has marshalled our collective trauma into
a world-wide trance,
~ today called the patriarchy.*

*Within this belief system,
women are marginalized,
as are people with skin of color.*

*This trance determines
who suffers and who flourishes.*

We are mired in its repetitive cruelty.

*A remedy for my weary soul,
~ a way out of its spellbinding grip ~
Is The Love I have found with
God the Mother."*
~ Shuna

As I sit at my keyboard and type the above thoughts, I can't shake the eerie feeling that I am breaking the rules. I fear that my words will be scorned by an unseen power that wants to keep my voice on a leash. Like women on every continent, I have been trained to do my own self-editing and stay "in my place" within the confines of my culture. I was taught to act a certain way, to look a certain way, and to serve the powers that be. Like many little girls growing up in the nineteen-sixties and seventies, I moved through the stages of my life immersed in the belief that my talents and dreams weren't nearly as important as the talents and dreams of little boys. When I mention this to family members, friends and colleagues, they often shrug and say, "That's just the way it is."

Only recently have I had the courage to take a direct and unflinching look at *how* the long history of the wounded masculine energies has silenced me. I realized that if I want to unleash a deeper experience of the Divine Feminine qualities within me ~ compassion, love, kindness, nurturing, intuition, presence ~ I first had to understand the invisible ways that the patriarchy has shaped and influenced me. I decided to search for and spotlight some of the *subtle* influences that patriarchal edicts have had on my soul.

A Tomboy

As a young girl, it was my nature to wade barefoot in the pond behind our house, catch frogs and listen to the endless flocks of red-winged blackbirds darting amongst the cattails. Each summer I played basketball and softball with neighborhood kids, and in the winter when the pond froze, I learned to sneak out of the house to play hockey with the boys ~ something my father did not approve of.

At age eight, as I raced my blue Schwinn bike through the neighborhood, an old man stood on his porch and laughed at me. "Hey!" he yelled. "You're such a tomboy!" I skidded to a stop in front of his picket fence and looked at him. I didn't know what to say because I didn't know what a tomboy was. But I could tell it wasn't good. I tucked my hair under my ball cap and headed home to ask mom.

Today, I wonder why an active, nature-loving girl is so casually given that label. How could I know this was designed to make me feel small? To superimpose a boy's name (Tom) and change my gender to boy? Calling me a "Tomboy" diminished the joy I felt just being me. With that label pinned to my chest, a fun-loving part of me retracted.

As an adult, I now pay more attention to our casual talk, and how our words focus attention on men and covertly disappear women. Here are a few examples I found . . .

When addressing a mixed crowd, we automatically use the words "man," and "guys," "boy" or "dude."

"Hey man, that movie was amazing!" or "Hey guys, let's order pizza." Or "Boy, I'm tired."

I used to brush these phrases off as insignificant. They aren't. I am not a man or a boy or a guy or a dude.

Regarding governments and organized religions, the following two examples summarize the influence that patriarchal beliefs have imbedded in our language:

"Father, Son and Holy Ghost."

"All men are created equal." (Note: Despite Abigail Adams's famous advice to her husband John Adams to "remember the ladies," he and the rest of the founders left any mention of women out of the founding documents.)

This is not trivial. This forms a young girl's self-image.

At Age Eleven, I Abandoned My Voice

I heard the words "feminist," and "patriarchy" on the same day, in a seventh-grade social studies class. Our teacher didn't tell us the meaning or social significance of these words, and our textbook didn't even mention them. Instead, I learned these words from a film he showed us that day. He started the projector and went back to his desk to read the newspaper.

Flickering on the screen was the headline "The New Feminists." I sat up, curious, and watched as a confident woman with long flowing hair and aviator glasses approached the podium. Her name appeared on the screen: Gloria Steinem. A crowd of thousands were gathered in front of the U.S Capitol to hear her speak. When she talked about equal rights for all people and how the "good old boys club" ~ she called it "the patriarchy" ~ was still silencing any voice challenging their power, they roared and raised their fists in defiance. I recall sitting up, excited, trying to hear her above the chatter behind me.

Boys in the back of the room were ridiculing her. "She just hates men," they taunted. "They all just hate men."

When I heard this, I sat up rigid and my face froze. This was the moment I abandoned my female voice and value. I fully understood that the opinion of boys and men far outweighed mine or Gloria's, so I hid my excitement. Since I didn't hate anybody, no way was I going to be one of those feminists.

Perhaps, if I had been taught in my high school history class about the burning of hundreds of thousands of women in the sixteenth century, I may have understood what Gloria and the other feminists were talking about. It wasn't until college, many years later, that I learned that the crime of these mostly peasant women was expressing their gifts as healers and intuitives, herbalists and midwives. Let's be honest, the Roman Catholic church didn't burn witches. They burned women ~ and also some men who expressed these same nurturing feminine qualities. Decades after college, I began to see the patriarchy as a deep wound in our collective consciousness, a wound that is still very active in the twenty-first century.

Soldiers or Servants

Every child born is required by their culture to become either soldiers or servants to this injurious trance. Little boys are expected to join its authoritarian power structure, and if they don't, they are marginalized. As an example, a man I've known since we were kids in the fourth grade has been bullied all his life because he is compassionate, nurturing and kind ~ characteristics of the feminine that are seen as weak. Little girls, on the other hand, aren't even invited to join the power structure. Instead, girls are gaslighted to believe their purpose is to serve and support the oppressive status quo.

Blame Eve

Every Sunday morning, I sat in our Lutheran church with my family ~ mother, father, sister and brother. My scraped eight-year-old legs would swing restlessly the entire time. I may have looked bored, but I was paying attention . . . I was curious about God, so during the sermon I'd scoot side to side on the polished wooden pew to get a better look at the pastor up front. He stood tall in his purple vestments and talked a lot about Father and Son. I heard those words repeated in the scripture he read, and the hymns we all sang. In my young mind I wondered ~ *Where is the mother and daughter? Why aren't we included in the church's family photo?* The more I listened to prayers and sermons and noticed the lyrics of the hymns, the more I couldn't tell if God even knew I was alive.

I learned that God was a man ~ a white man, actually ~ and he lived somewhere above us in the sky. From moment to moment, I didn't know what to expect from this God. Sometimes he was kind, and sometimes cruel. In one sermon I heard the pastor talk about God's wrath and eternal damnation. My eyes grew wide, and I went into some kind of shock. I leaned into my mom and said, "Mom, he's scaring me."

She pulled me closer and kept her eyes on the pulpit. "Shhh," she said. "It's OK, honey."

The most upsetting moment in my religious training was the day in Sunday school we were told about Adam and Eve. From this story I learned that women are to blame for all that is wrong with the world. A deep shame lodged in my chest ~ shame that I was a girl. Imagine the harm this story has done and is still doing to the innocent hearts of millions of little girls ~ and the dangerous message it sends to little boys.

LEGAL DISCRIMINATION BASED ON SEX

At sixteen, I had developed into a deep-thinking introvert, had a few close friends, and earned decent grades. I had learned to hide my intellect and opinions so I wouldn't offend anyone, and my only outlet was sports. Thank goodness for sports! I was consistently the high scorer on the girls' varsity basketball team. I loved the way my body felt when I sprinted down the court, and the seamless teamwork we used to rack up the points. We were undefeated for three years in a row and became regional champions.

The year was 1971, and sex discrimination was legal. Girls literally had no civil rights in the classroom or in athletics. Our success as athletes carried no weight. I include this backstory to contrast our championship status with the dismal season our football team was having.

One afternoon, we were in the middle of a practice scrimmage when the double doors to the gym flew open. "Hey girls, sorry to interrupt your practice, but it's pouring outside and we're gonna need the gym." The head football coach stood in his dripping rain poncho as his team gathered behind him in muddy pools of water, their cleats caked with dirt.

"You gotta leave so we can finish our drills," he continued. He was built like an aging linebacker, and had a look in his eye that said, *Everyone understands football is more important than any girls' team.*

I stood in my white converse high-tops with a basketball tucked under my arm, and looked at our coach, wondering what was going on.

The aging linebacker assumed we would leave, and frankly, I did too. We didn't question that the boys had the right to the gym. So, my teammates and I wiped our sweaty faces on our shirts and silently began to pick up all the loose basketballs.

A sharp blast on a whistle made us jump. Coach Danek dropped the whistle from her teeth, crossed her arms, and commanded, "Sit down, girls."

Of all the emotions I could have felt in that moment, my face flushed red with embarrassment. *What was she doing? Why was she making such a big deal about this? Didn't she know they were more important?* But we obeyed and sat together in the center of the court. When the boys saw this, they rolled their eyes, puffed their chests and tucked their helmets under their arms. Some of them jeered. It was tense. We sat in silence while the two coaches stepped in the hall to talk it out. Several of the boys made snide remarks under their breath and did a lot of laughing.

We huddled closer, wrapped our arms around our knees and said nothing.

When the coaches returned, the aging linebacker was storming mad and said to his team, "We're going to let them have the gym." The boys groaned and strode out in a huff. A couple of them flashed the bird as they exited.

We stood and threw our arms in the air, victorious. At that moment, part of me came back to life. A space of more freedom opened inside me. I felt small tremors of joy reverberate in my heart and belly. *So, this is how it feels to be as important as boys. This is what it's like to stand up for my rights.* But these thoughts were quickly followed by, *I wonder if we'll get into trouble.*

I'll never know how our coach found the courage and grit to challenge this intrusion. Maybe she was just fed up, maybe this was the hundredth time she had to submit to blatant discrimination. But she showed us we had the right to peacefully protest against injustice ~ a right we didn't know we had. She blew her whistle again and said, "Ok, let's get back to work."

The following year, 1972, Congress passed Title IX, prohibiting sex discrimination, into federal law.

I wish I could report that the federal law prohibiting sex discrimination did the trick, but turning the *Titanic* takes time. Today, fifty-four-years later, I see much of the same harmful messaging disparaging women or enticing them to give up their own dreams for another person. These messages are still written into modern movie scripts, lyrics of popular songs as well as in politics, the daily news, and on social media. The patriarchy still assumes a woman's purpose is to support the wounded masculine.

The good news is that women have gained some ground in Western culture! I am heartened to see younger women in their twenties, thirties and forties stepping into leadership positions more freely. This is surely progress for humanity! Yet I know my sisters in other parts of the world, their wings clipped, still suffer greatly.

Last summer, I was thinking about this as I pulled weeds in our dahlia garden. When I stood to stretch my back, I was struck with a sudden epiphany. *Wait a minute . . .Why am I waiting for permission from my wounded culture to tell me it's safe for me to express ~ and that my thoughts and opinions are welcomed and needed?* I pulled the gloves off my hands and proclaimed out loud, "I can give that permission to myself!"

To do this, I needed a plan. I knew it was on me to do the inner work to establish my own sense of being safe in the world. I settled into a daily meditation practice and established a relationship with plant medicines to usher me into deeper layers of my consciousness. This is where I received a better understanding of our human relationship with the Divine.

God the Mother

As I continued to evolve in my spiritual awareness, a presence began speaking to me during my meditations. It was not the voice of my courageous coach or an early feminist, or any person on the outside. It was God the Mother communicating with me from within. Over time, She has guided me to release the shame I still carried from the Adam and Eve story, and she has lovingly assured me that Mother and Daughter are indeed a vital presence in the family photo, alongside Father and Son.

Each morning, I make a cup of tea, wrap my purple shawl around my shoulders, and sit in my meditation chair. I light a candle and prepare to be present with Her once again. I am always delighted to sense her voice speaking clearly to my heart. On one particular morning, she had a lot to say:

> *"My dearest daughter, I am God the Mother, the spirit of the Divine Feminine. You are here at the behest of ancestors in your female lineage. They support you from beyond the veil to help transform the suffering of this world. This, dear daughter, is a call to embody your divinity. The Divine Feminine qualities of love, compassion, empathy and leadership that live in every soul, must now lead humanity out of its self-created darkness."*

One eye opened and I found my journal. She continued.

> "My dear daughter, you are here to join with others who challenge the old ways of thinking that cause human and planetary suffering. As a species, and as a living planetary system, you are at a precipice.
>
> Don't be fooled into thinking the trance of patriarchy is about men winning. It isn't. In this trance, everyone loses. Many women are now finding their voice and claiming their place in the herstory of humanity. Also, each day, more men tire of the tyranny promoted by patriarchal values and are inviting Me into their heart."

Then, radio silence. Her words just stopped. I took a deep breath, hyper-aware of this moment. I brushed my silver hair behind my ears and willed myself to stay deep in my expanded mind, wanting to remember every word. I waited. Eventually I said out loud, "How can I help?"

As though waiting for me to speak, She replied,

> "Know this ~ Words have the power to inspire and motivate. Speak your words, dear daughter ~ of love and unity. Speak your words into the ethers. Gather in alliance with those of like mind, and with your ancestors ~ the women and men who contributed their ovum and seed for countless generations to make your life possible. You who walk on Earth today, and breathe her atmosphere, are their hope.
>
> This is a clarion call from the Divine Feminine, from God the Mother. Know that I dearly love you as you are. You are a sacred being. You are ~ and always have been ~ the light, dearly beloved."

When I felt Her love, I was stunned to realize I never trusted the white male god promoted by the patriarchal religions. He is not what has been endorsed by religious dogma. The god of my early years in church fell away.

To be clear, I don't see God the Mother as a woman. Spirit has no gender. Instead, She blesses us with the feminine qualities that are needed to bring balance to the human heart. She taught me we also have Divine Masculine qualities in us that are meant to support and create a safe environment for the life-enhancing leadership of the Divine Feminine. The Divine Masculine within us is a foundational and practical energy that is stable, confident, steadfast and protective. However, in these times, our Divine Masculine energies have been muted by the persistent cruelty of the wounded masculine.

A REMEDY?

Is there a remedy, a medicine or change in our mindset that can heal the ills of centuries of gender and racial oppression? Yes, I believe there is. Our sacred task is to unshackle the Divine Masculine energies within us so it can support our Divine Feminine to nurture compassion and love in the human heart.

Today, when I look in the mirror, I see a rebel elder and wise woman with silver hair and clear green eyes smiling back at me. All of who I am ~ the elder; the bike-racing, nature-loving girl; the girl who wanted to know God; the girl who felt a stirring in her heart when she learned of feminists and the patriarchy; and the girl who learned how to sit on the basketball court for her rights ~ is claiming her rightful place as a compassionate leader in a hurting world. Now that my Divine Masculine is supporting and protecting the natural expression of my Divine Feminine, I'm thrilled to say, I have found my Voice.

About Shuna Morelli MS, LMT, CH

Shuna Morelli MS, LMT, CH has a master's degree in science education and is the author of five books. She has had a life-long intrigue and curiosity about the seamless connection of body and mind. Shuna has developed and teaches a system of self-healing known as BodyMind Bridge, which accesses an expanded level of consciousness.

It was during her own BodyMind Bridge meditations that she first met the feminine aspect of the Divine. This has been pivotal to her healing from the oppressive culture of wounded masculine energies that envelop our Mother Earth. It is her desire that more women recognize the fog of patriarchy surrounding them and begin their own quest to meet the divine spiritual power within them.

Website: **Shunamorelli.com**

Chapter 9

ASHES FORGIVEN: THE LONG SHADOW OF SIBLING RAPE

Angie Merritt

Today, I held my brother's ashes... encased in a plastic bag within a cardboard box. It is with mixed feelings that I say goodbye because of the complex relationship we had over my 75 years. Fear sometimes, irritation sometimes, but also deep empathy and frustration that I could not help him more. Here is my prayer that came forth for his healing:

I heal your heart, your abandoned, sad, cross-purposed heart.
I plug the leak with love-glue and your beloved cats.
I see you with your obesity tamed, your hunger sated,
Your insight at work rewarded and appreciated,
Your starvation for affection filled,
Your overwhelmingly chaotic house cleared,
Your love for your sons returned,
Your body once again responsive, agile, and manageable,
Your mind once again sharp and your tongue clever,
A proper Southern gentleman of the 1950s attained,
You are healed. And so am I.

The perspective that age brings is a great gift. Looking back at a whole life with contours of ups and downs, struggles and victories, allows insights not available during the journey itself. What caused what? What led to what? The past is more understandable to me now.

Angie Merritt

What follows are our stories.

In my good Southern church-going upbringing, girls were supposed to be polite and not cause trouble. My mother would tell me every time I left the house "Be sweet." I was never introduced to setting boundaries. In our cotton mill town, my classmates in public school were raised with similar standards, and I never had a need for such discussions. So, I was "sweet." It was a more innocent time and place for me.

Sex was never discussed. When, as a child, I questioned my mother about the mysterious bundles wrapped in newspaper in her trash can, I got a terse "sanitary napkins" with no further explanation. I was introduced to menstruation by a booklet left in my bedroom. I developed earlier than some of my classmates and had budding breasts before them. I was introduced to training bras by my friends six months before I was supplied with a bra. My parents' bedroom door stayed open all the time.

Flash back to 1960. It was a sweltering summer night and I was visiting my grandparents, a usual weekly family activity. Sometimes there were cousins to play with, but mostly I sat and listened to the adults talk to each other ~ no special kids' entertainment or toys provided. Children really were expected to be seen and not heard.

That night, my brother, who was about 5 years older than I, invited me out to the car while the adults talked about people I didn't know. I was a tween, breast buds just blooming. I thought he wanted to teach me how to drive. He was crazy about cars. He did want to show me something. He said it was something most girls didn't learn until they were older. That was enticing as I was a smart, eager learner, full of curiosity. It turned out he wanted to fondle me, finger up my privates. It was not fun, not the education I wanted, and not welcome. Flash again to a hot afternoon later that fall with the light pouring into my bedroom from the western sun... when I was held down by my hair and raped by him when I refused to play his games again. Being overpowered was as scary as the entry was painful.

I didn't have a word for it. I didn't know telling was an option. Sex wasn't an acceptable topic in my household. He was my brother; I had no idea what the outcome would be if I told. What I decided was that this was what people talked about when they said girls couldn't be as free as boys to come and go and needed to be protected. But I was in my own home. My solution was to protect myself. I arranged never to be alone with my brother again. My parents never knew until years later. If I couldn't trust my brother, whom I loved, then I couldn't trust men at all. Maybe I couldn't trust anyone.

Thus began the subconscious forces in my life that made me feel invisible, voiceless, powerless over others, and reluctant to trust.

I proceeded with life. I was not a social butterfly in high school. I was smart, involved, and successful, but never asked to the prom or on dates. This was before girls asked guys. I think I must have given off an air of *leave me alone*.

I went to a mostly girls' college, which was fine by me. During freshman orientation at University of North Carolina at Greensboro, busloads of girls were hauled to UNC Chapel Hill to meet freshmen boys. Down one side of the valley came the girls to meet with boys coming down the other side of the valley. Everyone was pairing up and going off to a football game.

Everyone but me.

I got to the bottom of the hill and looked around for who might be left and discovered... no one was left. I was miserable, wondering what was the matter with me, while I had to wait lonely hours for the buses to reload.

Throughout college, I studied hard. I was active, made good friends – all girls – and graduated cum laude. I got a fellowship to graduate school in Chapel Hill. While there, I had relationships with two men, both of whom were older, married, and safe. They were kind initiators. I learned sex could be nice. I met my future husband, who was so incompetent, he felt safe, kind of like Woody Allen with less charm and less capability of producing an income.

I won a fellowship to study in Colombia, South America for a year. We married and drove to Panama, then sold the car and flew to Colombia. It was a grand adventure. After a school year in a Colombian University, we moved to the countryside and stayed another six months. It was mind opening to experience another culture in a day-to-day way.

Coming back to the United States was a culture shock. All that education and no one tells you how to get a job. I got one, but my husband didn't. My 'Woody Allen' husband found everything suitable to his real skills beneath his dignity. He was increasingly hard to deal with.

Two kids later, we moved back to my hometown to have a little back up to raise them, and things got increasingly worse. I was the only one working, and caring for two children *and* my irrational husband sucked all my energy. He criticized me for everything. According to him I couldn't even talk to a friend on the phone right.

I fell back into believing God was available to help. I wrote a lot of prayers and discovered prayer is especially useful for adjusting my own attitude. I looked for the high road in dealing with the chaos he caused constantly.

When the boys started school, it turned out that they both had several learning disabilities. It was all too much. I couldn't keep the boat afloat and help them if my husband took up all my time and energy. I was taught marriage was forever, so I believed I must deal with it. I remember feeling sick to my stomach for weeks as I came to the decision that I had to get rid of him to concentrate on helping my boys. And I longed to have space to just be and not be under constant attack.

I finally ran away from the home that we shared, trying to get him to leave. It was *my* house, an old rental in a rough part of town that my parents had given me. He tracked me down and wouldn't leave. He lived in his truck in my yard for 6 months, habitually breaking into my house to shower and wash clothes. On Veterans' Day, it snowed. I had time to have him arrested since I was off work for the holiday. I was afraid he would be in real danger as winter came.

He finally went to his mother's house. I was never sure he wouldn't come back and take my younger son. He didn't want my older son who was developing some of his father's mental health issues. My husband was later diagnosed with bipolar disorder, but at the time, I just wondered how other couples manage to make marriage work. So much for picking a safe man. The long shadow of sibling rape is evident.

I struggled with the devastation of 17 years of emotional and psychological abuse from my mentally ill husband on top of my rape trauma. My self-esteem was the lowest of my life. My lack of voice, my invisibility and powerlessness, and my inability to deeply trust others all made my life a desperate struggle.

At work, I struggled to hold my own and do the job. I got fired and had to start over in a new job. I was too wounded to even think about a new relationship. I had a lot of healing to do.

Then I got a direct message from God to try out for a role in *Fiddler on the Roof* with our tiny local theater. I'd seen the movie on television and been drawn to it. When auditions were announced, I heard the message "Go do it." It was the first of many plays, as I found I loved being on stage and having roles. Through acting, I began to gain confidence in myself. It was the beginning of healing my voice.

My brother's experience was different growing up. When he was three, our mother had tuberculosis and was sent to the sanitorium for eighteen months. This was the cure before antibiotics: cold air in the short months of winter, bed rest, and injections of air into her lungs.

My father had to work to pay for her treatment so he farmed his little boy out to aunts and uncles on both sides of the family, especially to our grandparents. Our grandfather was an outgoing man who could talk to anyone, so my brother learned to talk to anyone. This was in the mid-40s in the rural south. Those disruptions in his life and the social environment left their marks on him.

My brother was an astute judge of character and the social and economic pressures behind people's behaviors. He could describe the essence of a story like the best of southern authors. Ironically, his name... Charles Dickens. He was entrepreneurial and willing to work. But he was not happy and struggled with depression from his teen years.

As a young man, my brother raced cars, legally and not, dated lots of young women in several counties, and worked at the local paper mill, which was hot and exhausting physical work. On his third try at college, he completed a 2-year business degree and took a job with the railroad. The railroad higher-ups evidently hated him because he could read the rule book and called them on it.

He eventually met a young lady, Linda, whose Japanese mother had pulled her out of high school to study cosmetology so she could support herself quickly. Her mother was dying of cancer caused by exposure to the bomb at Hiroshima. Her stepfather was abusive in every way possible: sexually, physically, emotionally, even stalking her after she moved out. My brother married her to protect her.

They adopted two boys. My brother was a surprisingly attentive father and diligent about teaching them practical skills, vocabulary, and his unusually perceptive insight into people and the factors that influence them.

Over the years, his wife became increasingly disabled by diabetes, mental health issues, and hoarding. There was only a narrow path through their house to essential areas: the bed, one bathroom, and a small part of the kitchen. My brother got fired from the railroad just before he could receive retirement. He opened a pawn shop. Linda lost a leg to diabetes and died after years in a nursing home.

Thirty years changes a person. I no longer felt I had to avoid being alone with him. I had witnessed his struggles and saw him being an attentive, loving parent; a coping husband; a thoughtful, insightful person with his coworkers; and a son who visited and loved our parents. He was considerate of me and my struggles. We were family ~ and family meant something.

Meanwhile, I was raising my boys and working. School was difficult for my smart but learning-disabled kids who could not read, write, or do math. They were also mad at me for getting rid of their father. Although they loved me, they often treated me with disrespect learned from their father ~ both verbal confrontation and lack of cooperation. I couldn't count on them to get themselves to school after I got them up and left for work 30 miles away. I had neither the skills nor the backup to govern teenage boys who didn't want to be governed. Neither graduated from high school. I received no child support, of course.

During these rough years, for whatever twisted reason, my ex called my parents from his mother's house to tell them I had been raped by my brother. I had to deal with the question of forgiveness again. A principle of Christianity that made sense to me was that I need to forgive if I want God to forgive me. Forgiving others opens the door for forgiving yourself and self-compassion. I could see no good coming from hostility towards my brother, so for his sake, my parents, or my own, I forgave him.

Fifteen years later, after a short-lived marriage to a narcissist, I married a good man who was no longer interested in an exciting life. I retired from my work with the school system and became a yoga teacher. My older son had died tragically, shot by his brother. He had inherited the mental illness of his father and became aggressive at times. Unable to escape, his brother shot him. It was determined to be self-defense.

I cared for my mother as she aged, until she died at 96. I grew emotionally, spiritually, and culturally. I learned new practices that build resilience and equanimity: yoga, meditation, pranayama, the daily habits of ayurveda, Taichi, qigong, Reiki, and other spiritual perspectives and traditions beyond the Christianity I had relied on for six decades of my life.

I also found myself caring for my husband through his ten-year journey through dementia, lung cancer, and his final decline after Covid. The deeper his dementia became, the lonelier I felt. I no longer had someone to share things with. His PTSD left him fearful of even going out to eat. It fell to me to cook for him, to supply his books until he could no longer read, to see that the television was on so he could watch the news all day, and to listen to the stories of his childhood over and over.

Simultaneously, due to my brother's increasing disability from Parkinson's and dementia, I became his caregiver. I don't mean that I changed his diapers, but I found him an assisted living facility, looked after his money, bought his diapers and snacks, took him to doctors' appointments, and was his only visitor. His sons were unconcerned, and while one son always wanted money, neither took any responsibility, seldom visiting without major prodding from me. He lived in his recliner, becoming increasingly unable to stand, feed himself, or otherwise care for himself. He got, and survived, Covid late in the pandemic, but declined quickly and went into Hospice care. He faded bit by bit and was never able to hold a conversation again.

Both my husband and my brother died within six months of each other, each shortly before his eightieth birthday.

My mother's death left me an orphan, and I had to step up into the role of matriarch of our tiny clan.

My husband's death left me a widow, but his long dementia had left me equipped to deal with being alone.

My brother's death left me the last one standing, with no one left to ask questions about our past. My grief for him is the tenderest, causing me to tear up often.

As a yogini, I know that death is part of life. Thinking people shouldn't die is just an invitation to more suffering. Their death is *their* story; it's not about me. My brother's death is sad for me because for 75 years I watched him struggle with life... and was unable to do anything about it. I could work on *my* life, not his. His raping me was a symptom of his own unhappiness and struggle as a teen. I think he expected cooperation from me in that sexual encounter, and in his frustration, forced me. I forgive him, even now, after a lifetime of being voiceless, invisible, unable to exert control over others, and reluctance to trust. That deep heart attachment was not destroyed by his betrayal.

I know, intellectually, that he got off light. We need to teach men, especially our young men, that the damage they cause by rape, molestation and violence lasts a lifetime to their victims. They steal our ability to use our innate gifts for the world at our highest capacity. Sibling sexual abuse is one of the most common forms of child sexual abuse.

I was not brutally raped by a stranger, or an invading army, or repeatedly by a family member. I had some control in being able to avoid my rapist in my teen years. But damage was done.

It is not the event, but our reaction to it, that causes us to be in trauma. Trauma is an experience that overwhelms our ability to process it. It damages our physical body. Trauma can be held in our cells and tissues and cause pain and disease. Trauma can be in our energy channels, disrupting flow and causing blockages that lead to disease and impaired life skills. Trauma leaves emotional scars in our mind that cause responses to come from our subconscious and lead to our reactions based on fear and untrue thoughts.

Damage was done in my root chakra, at the rape site. It is the center that supports our belief in our right to take up space in the world, be seen…to *BE*.

Damage was also done to my throat chakra in suppressing a deep truth when I did not feel free to tell. I am still learning to speak my truth and to believe anyone will listen. Asking for what I want is still a challenge.

Damage was done to my heart chakra, putting up a wall to possibilities of getting close, a self-protective shield. Once past the shield, I can have deep relationships, but allowing that entry is difficult for me.

We develop scars in our mind that influence our patterns of behavior. We see the world through a filter that influences each experience in front of us.

Each damaged area needs healing. Yoga helps enormously to move energy through the stuck places in our body. Meditation helps our mind scars. Therapy, coaching, energy work, hypnosis, counseling, Emotional Freedom Technique or tapping, and *The Work* of Byron Katie, just to name a few, can help us see the truth beyond our limited thought patterns. We *can* learn new behaviors.

Unforgiveness keeps us stuck. Forgiveness is a gift we can give to ourselves. It does not mean we have to let others in where they can hurt us again. It has to do with compassion and seeing that the transgression came from pain and ignorance. I think people are doing the best they can at any moment given what they know, considering the pain deep in their bodies and minds that sets up patterns of behavior.

Realizing how my traumas damaged me makes me more empathetic to others and how damage from their own life experiences can affect them. I aspire to help people regulate their nervous systems through my work as a yoga and meditation teacher, reiki practitioner, energy coach, holistic health educator, and as an accepting human being.

Now, living alone in my 70s, I feel so powerful in the sovereignty of my being, and truly blessed to finally be able to creatively live my best life. And... I have a satisfying sex life with a new boyfriend!

We are never too old to learn, grow and change. Just because we have always been stuck in our ways doesn't mean we can't learn, heal and grow into our 60s and beyond. We believe our thoughts, assuming they are *truth*, but it's our brain seeing patterns. We *can* become happier, and life can work better by changing our beliefs. If you find yourself less happy than you'd like, even as an older adult, seek help.

Change is *always* possible.

About Angie Merritt

After a lifetime of meaningful work and after losses and tragedies, Angie has friends who call her the 'Queen of Resilience.' Now in her mid-70s, she lives with her two cutie dogs and standoffish cat in her childhood home in a small Southern town. She continues to grow and learn through travel, audiobooks, growing her entrepreneurial skills, and studying the wisdom of other cultures.

Her current vision is to lead other seniors to become intentional agers so they can give their gifts and live their dreams. She does this through movement, habits of health, mindset and energy work. Her yoga teaching and wisdom can be experienced on her YouTube channel at *Age Well Health Quest*.

Angie's gift to you: her story of learning from the tragedy of her son's death, "Beauty for Ashes."

Email her at JoyfulVitalityyoga@gmail.com with "Beauty for Ashes" in the subject line and she will share it with you

Chapter 10

WHAT DOES LOVE LOOK LIKE HERE?

Liz Turnbull, LMT

*"When life is sweet, say thank you and celebrate.
When life is bitter, say thank you and grow."*
~ Shauna Niequist

This is the story of the beginning of the end of my family. I have few memories of ever feeling safe with my family. I spent most of my youth feeling that it was too unsafe to inhabit my body, so I didn't.

I lived in my head and in fantasy as much as possible. I remember spending much of my spare time reading or playing outdoors. I especially loved being out in nature, imagining myself living countless adventures. I felt less vulnerable alone in the woods of British Columbia with mountain lions than I did in the presence of my family.

Healing from injuries from a car accident in my early twenties forced me to slowly and steadily learn how to live in my body again. Embodiment made me aware of many painful experiences and complicated traumas. Surviving in a family riddled with addictions, abuse, and tons of unhealed trauma is rough.

To live a healthy and happy life, I had to change what was happening. No matter how hard the process might be, I had to figure out how to feel again in order to heal and grow.

Liz Turnbull

DIVING DEEP

*"Courage is very important. Like a muscle,
it's strengthened by use."*
~ Ruth Gordon

With the support of therapists, healers, and friends, I've spent over three decades healing and learning invaluable self-care techniques. I learned how to process the abuse my body retained with yoga, tai chi, mindfulness meditation, physiological psychotherapy, and therapeutic bodywork.

In my twenties, I started really seeing that my family was riddled with some pretty unhealthy and dysfunctional patterns. I soon realized that healing had to start with me, the only person I could truly change.

I was just over a year old when my birth father started physically abusing me. He experienced intense rage when stressed, a family legacy going back at least a few generations. He would beat me for having diarrhea which was caused by food allergies. He was finishing medical school while my mom was supporting us all as a nurse, so there was lots of stress. Mom was also going through medical testing and procedures for her autoimmune disease which had flared up after my birth. In my thirties, after I shared some experiences in therapy that confused me, Mom told me about the abuse.

Due to my parents' school and work schedule, I was often at my paternal grandparents' house, where my uncle began sexually abusing me when I was about 18 months old. When I was 3 years old, my mother worked up the courage and filed for divorce. She was scorned and abandoned by family on both sides because the community frowned upon divorce.

After multiple attempted kidnappings, my birth father lost visitation rights with my sister and me. Subsequently, my birth father stopped paying child support and we were adopted by Mom's second husband. Sadly, my adoptive father also struggled with anger issues, addictions, and was abusive.

I started going through perimenopause in my mid-forties and the changes gave rise to more anger than I knew I could handle. The rage was terrifying rather than empowering because it would explode, like a monster erupting in me, with an intensity that overwhelmed me.

Once, a large Ford truck sped through a four-way stop, missing me by mere feet. A surge of rage overtook me and I began screaming at the top of my lungs. Something monstrous took control of my body, pushing me aside as it floored the gas pedal, and with a death grip on the steering wheel, recklessly sped after the truck, intent on ramming it.

I came out of this suicidal rage and stopped just before impact. I started shaking and broke into hysterical tears on the side of the road. I realized I was as much a danger to myself as others were, if not more. I felt so conflicted, hurt, scared, angry and hopelessly overwhelmed that I started hitting myself and pulling out my hair.

My therapist called it infantile rage, a pre-verbal trauma response that we later linked to sexual and physical abuse that I had experienced in my youth (especially the incidents when I was an infant and toddler).

I worked for years with a therapist trained in body-focused trauma psychotherapy. In these sessions, I courageously opened up to a legion of repressed and unprocessed psychological and physical traumas from my past (sexual and physical abuse, kidnapping, car accidents, and complex psychological abuse).

In one of the sessions, we focused on chronic pain in my lower back and hip. As I held awareness of the pain with a sense of curiosity, I started remembering the terror of being violently injured in an auto accident when I was 22. The other car ran a red light and hit the driver's door, sending me and my seat up over the passenger seat. The other driver took off and left me and my roommate in my totaled VW bug. I suffered head trauma, a dislocated jaw and many soft tissue injuries.

As the memories came back, the therapist asked me, "What would your body have liked to have done to protect you back then?" It would have liked to have seen the other car first, hit the brakes and swerved to avoid it. The therapist told me to turn his hands like the steering wheel and push my foot on the floor like a brake, so I did. I started shaking and crying. The therapist calmly held the space for me to process these long-trapped emotions finally set free. Healing this chronic pain required multiple sessions that helped me process all of the remnants of years and years of physical and sexual abuse that I held as tension in these parts of my body.

I survived so much abuse by separating my awareness from feeling anything too overwhelming. My body retained the unprocessed emotions so I could keep functioning but it was only a temporary solution. Unfelt and unreleased traumas lead to disease and dysfunction. Despite all I've experienced up to now, this part of my healing journey took the most courage I've ever mustered.

To be able to thrive, I knew I had to release all of these traumatic bindings and reclaim my spirit and my vitality. The sheer number of times and ways that my dysfunctional family system had harmed me was so overwhelming, I often wanted to stop this emotionally challenging healing work. Still, I knew in my gut that all of the pain needed to be acknowledged, felt, and released for me to flourish. Bit by bit, I began healing and growing healthier.

Over time, I clearly saw the web of unresolved traumas trapping my family members in their harmful behaviors. I realized that when we are unable and/or unwilling to process and heal trauma, we keep ourselves and each other trapped in unhealthy connections, relying on harmful coping mechanisms like numbing, manipulating, distracting, controlling and blaming, to name a few. In trying to avoid suffering, we only create more suffering.

Using the 12-step program for Codependency, I focused on my own healing and worked to set strong boundaries while still providing love and care for my disabled mother. Detaching with love and healing old wounds is challenging and takes effort, so I understand why so many people decide not to do it.

With support from friends and professionals, I have repeatedly found the courage to keep healing. I continue to recover from past abuse and have learned to accept that I can't help loved ones unless they're ready to help themselves.

Understanding my family members' wounds has at least helped me to feel compassion for and forgive them for the harms they caused me. I've apologized and attempted to make amends, when appropriate, for the harms I caused. This has helped heal some relationships and I'm always hopeful about the others. Now, I am committed to healthier relationships and no longer putting myself at risk from the unhealthy ones.

My commitment to boundaries, nonviolent communication, honesty, and compassion has permanently changed my family's dysfunctional dynamics. I've stepped out of my role as a codependent enabler and can now more gracefully ride the crazy waves my dysfunctional family system still creates.

Liz Turnbull

Crazy Wave Surfing

*"If you're not riding the waves of change,
you'll find yourself beneath them."*
~ unknown

I worked hard at keeping my integrity and compassion intact during the last years of my parents' lives. I mastered surfing crazy waves while living through my menopausal transition. I was committed to being a healthy ally to my parents as they took their last, not-so-graceful laps in life.

My mother was severely disabled by autoimmune disease and began relying on me when I was just 4 years old. I promised to take care of her when she was diagnosed with Lupus, right before her second marriage. Mom received little support from my father, who resented caretaking. As her condition worsened, both of my parents' dependence on me grew.

My parents were both addicts who were highly functional in their professional lives, but very destructive in their personal lives. They frequently abused multiple substances which led to a lot of illness, emotional and financial stressors, and fighting.

My father's substance abuse reached a dangerous peak in his early seventies. I called for an intervention after seeing him return to work as a psychiatrist after drinking two bottles of wine at lunch. My brother and his wife flew in, and the family sat down with him and talked to him about our observations and fears. He got very angry, telling us he was fine. I brought up my fears about endangering his patients and himself ~ and he said he could cut back on his own and walked out. My sister-in-law spoke with my brother back at their hotel about how there was no way that would work, so he called my recovering addict sister (15 years sober) from across the country.

They managed to convince Dad and he reluctantly entered a six-week rehab program for physicians but refused the 12-step and psychological work. Mom stopped drinking but barely engaged with the 12-steps, adding to their strained dynamic.

Dad had lots of unresolved trauma that started when he was 18 months old. He was sent alone on a ship from England to Canada during WWII to escape bombings. For weeks, he was one of hundreds of children cared for by a handful of overwhelmed nurses. In Canada, he was pampered by his wealthy relatives but returned at age 5 to a war-torn England, a struggling family, and siblings he'd never met. His mother relied on him emotionally and blamed him for his brother's suicide, though he was just 22 and away at medical school when it happened. Despite mental illness and addiction in the family, he believed he didn't need therapy.

The 12-step program for codependency helped me to accept the truth that the only real power I had was to focus on my own healing and well-being while helping my parents. The most complicated part for me was discerning the best approach as my parents' behavior became increasingly more dysfunctional. After about 10 years, Dad's substance abuse intensified, leading to more dangerous and destructive behaviors. He was often angry and belligerent, drinking and driving, and physically hostile.

When things got really dangerous physically and financially, my mother finally filed for divorce (specifically to protect at least one-half of their retirement savings from my father's risky behaviors). My parents continued to live together through their divorce. My mother stayed committed to their partnership but my father felt betrayed and spiraled into increasingly more frightening Mr. Hyde-like behavior patterns (addiction fueled waves of rage, violent outbursts, and manipulative behaviors).

I found healthy ways to stay engaged with them: I communicated my needs clearly and set firm boundaries on what was acceptable behavior. I took good care of myself whenever necessary, which often meant removing myself from the situation until acceptable behaviors were resumed.

Despite being endangered by Dad's intoxicated rages, Mom refused assisted living. Eventually, we moved her to a retirement community with extra help. After a winter storm left Dad without heat or power, Mom convinced him to move into the same complex.

My parents shared meals and watched TV together, appearing comfortable on the surface. However, their volatile relationship and unhealthy dynamics persisted, though now from the safer distance of separate apartments.

As Dad kept drinking and raging, and Mom kept trying to manipulate and control as much as possible, I kept detaching with love and orienting myself by asking myself, "What does love look like here?"

How do I act from healthy love with a violent, angry, intoxicated parent? One example was when Dad asked me to come with him to see a symphony performance. I said, "I'd love to if we can go sober." because his unpredictable behavior was always stressful for me, especially in public. He got angry with me and never asked again.

How do I show healthy love to a frightened codependent enabler parent? Mom kept trying to get me to go and clean my Dad's apartment because he was living in mounds of trash and abandoned food. She knew he could get kicked out if it got bad enough. I talked with them both and we finally agreed that he'd pay Mom's helper to come clean once a week.

How do I show myself love while engaging with an entire family system that dances almost exclusively to the tunes of denial, anger, and fear? I pay close attention to how I am feeling and do what I need to in order to take proper care of myself. The first time Mom got angry with me for refusing to return to codependent enabling behaviors, I went home, cried and then did 20 minutes of Yoga Nidra. Then, after finishing up my own work and housekeeping responsibilities, I watched a stand-up comedian and called a friend for support.

Sadly, Mom stayed angry about my consistent refusal to engage in codependent behaviors until the day she died. Understanding the difference between helping and enabling helped me accept her anger without taking it personally. I still managed to show up compassionately for her without taking on what wasn't mine.

Being open to and curious about the pain behind all of my family's unhealthy behavior was how I held onto love. It allowed me to find understanding and compassion for all of us. Regardless, I was not going to accept or excuse unacceptable behaviors, so I also used psychotherapist and author David Richo's priceless relationship wisdom: "I take care of myself but not at the expense of others, and I take care of others but not at the expense of myself."

I started preparing myself for the challenge of accompanying them as they grew closer to their deaths. I loved them, but knew they were hazardous for me. They were like drowning people who, in a panic, try to climb onto their rescuer and end up drowning everyone. My other family members had their own family and health issues or were far away, so I had to figure out how to be their sole caretaker without them taking me down with them.

I am committed to balancing self-care and other-care as much as possible. I practiced the 12 steps, acknowledged and nurtured my own needs, and learned about "Conscious Dying" (how to prepare physically, emotionally and spiritually) from an indigenous wisdom elder.

I found it all very emotionally and physically challenging. Still, I kept showing up even though I often thought about getting as far away from my dysfunctional family as possible. I always felt that there was something important about continuing to relate using all of the healthy relationship tools and self-care that I had been collecting. More than anything, I wanted to continue showing up in healthy ways with love.

In March 2020, the COVID-19 pandemic hit, bringing an overwhelming wave of chaos. Unresolved traumas on a global scale made the stress of the pandemic even more devastating, creating a tsunami of pain and fear on an unprecedented scale for all of us.

The retirement facility banned outside care workers and visitors, so tasks previously handled by Mom's helper fell to me. Overwhelmed by fear and the loss of control, we all took things one day at a time. The stress brought out the worst in Dad and his mental and physical health declined quickly due to his worsening substance abuse. It was especially stressful having to meet with the retirement complex director because Dad was sneaking out during quarantine to buy alcohol. He was almost evicted but we managed to convince him to comply by delivering his alcohol to prevent withdrawal.

During the pandemic, my father's anger fueled his substance abuse, which spiraled into liver failure and hospitalization. My mother's health rapidly declined. She suffered from multiple painful and disabling disorders and needed help with nearly every aspect of daily life.

At a particularly tough moment, I had to choose between continuing my caretaking role or supporting a dear friend as she laid her wife's ashes to rest. I chose to honor my friends. Thankfully, my sister was newly vaccinated (with 15 years of the gifts of sobriety under her belt) and was able to fly across the country to take over for the week.

When Dad was released from the hospital on hospice, my sister asked if he had a will. He didn't, so with witnesses present, he expressed his wish to split his estate among his five children. She used a template to draft a will, which he signed. He passed away five days later.

We discovered Dad had left Mom as the beneficiary of his accounts. Though she initially agreed to honor his will, she later decided to keep everything. I explained to her that doing so would irreparably damage our relationship since it was his love language and last wish. Reluctantly, she signed most of it over to his estate but spent the rest of her life resenting me for enforcing that boundary.

Soon after his death, Mom was diagnosed with lung cancer and placed on hospice care. Hospice's kindness and support were invaluable. As the retirement facility partially reopened, her helper organized a care team that helped me cope when Mom deteriorated and needed 24/7 care. At one terrifying point, we couldn't get her morphine because of supply chain problems, but these amazing nurses found some and collected it from close to 100 miles away.

Each day, I dug deep to show up, focusing on self-care and asking, "What does love look like here?" I faced relentless waves of fear, anger, frustration, and grief amid the pandemic's chaos. With a loving community and self-care, I found the strength to endure this hell on earth, one day at a time.

EMBRACING THE END & LETTING GO WITH LOVE

> *"The greatest gift we can give to the world is creating a continuous, uninterrupted, loving family structure."*
> ~ Aldona Laita

Navigating the chaos required courage, awareness, and surrender ~ embracing the flow of life and letting go. Looking back, I can see I was releasing a family I deeply loved. They were wonderful people at their best but too trapped in unresolved traumas to function in any healthy way.

Ironically, my parents, as mental health professionals, introduced me to deep emotional work but didn't use it for their own healing. When we do the work to process our traumas and heal, we free ourselves and each other from harmful ways of relating. We are no longer trapped and drowning in the emotional chaos of unresolved pain and suffering.

By courageously diving deep, uncovering unhealed trauma, and bringing it into the light with love, we heal. From those deeply healed places, all of our gifts can finally shine. Healthy relationships become possible as we learn to joyfully ride the waves of life and change together.

Through all of these challenges, I have found my center and a deep sense of my agency, needs, desires, strengths and weaknesses. From this sense of groundedness, I am able to act with integrity and intention. I now possess so many hard-earned and necessary skills for handling challenging tasks in my own life and for helping others. I feel especially blessed to be able to help people who are healing from trauma and many health issues. I gained so much wisdom to share on my healing journeys. Helping people learn healthy and effective behaviors and communication skills makes me tremendously happy.

I've also found a strong sense of belonging in this interconnected story of life. I have an incredible community full of found family and allies. We are all invested in healthy lives and relationships. We treat each other with great respect and consideration, addressing conflicts and challenges with compassion, curiosity, cooperation and healthy communication skills. It is my greatest hope that we all find our way out of pain and fear and into healthy relationships that buoy us all with support, hope and love.

ABOUT LIZ TURNBULL, LMT

Liz Turnbull, LMT is passionate about health and healing, spirituality, and the arts. She enjoys learning and growing.

She's written for Essence of Life magazine, some newsletters and has chapters in several books, including Alzheimer's Disease: A Handbook for Caregivers and Goddess Gift: Discover Your Personal Goddess Type.

Liz is a Licensed Massage Therapist and bodyworker with close to 3 decades of experience. She has been recognized for her volunteer work with the Multiple Sclerosis Society and various AIDS projects in North Carolina and Tennessee.

Liz co-created and managed a website devoted to archetypal psychology, **www.goddessgift.com**, that features mythology and the popular Goddess Quiz. She's a regular contributor to The Goddess Gift e-zine.

Liz teaches communication skills and the 'human side of health care' to physicians and other health care professionals in an award-winning program that uses simulated patients and professionals to improve interviewing and inter-professional skills.

Devoting much of her spare time to developing a website offering health focused e-courses, workshops and seminars, Liz enjoys spending time reading or hiking in the magnificent mountains of Northeast Tennessee.

Gift: **www.knowingandhealing.com**
Plus: a guided meditation on Inanna

Chapter 11

MEDEA, THE MOTHER AND ME

Vajra Ma

PRELUDE

I literally cannot stand up. I feel like I am smashed to the seafloor with the entire weight of the ocean bearing down on me. The performance of my one-woman show is scheduled for two weeks from NOW and I don't have a finished script.

I've always been impulsive. This time my impulse was to get the musicians, director, venue and performance date before I had a finished script. I figured, erroneously, it would accelerate my completion of the script.

How did I get here in this undersea paralysis? This was more than my usual procrastination. Much more. I had to figure it out. And fast!

I decided to hole myself up for three days and emerge with a finished script, one I would then have to craft as an actress. It is one thing to write a play, quite another to *act* it.

Accomplishing this was becoming a major "act of power" ~ *an action that converts subconscious material and fear into conscious awareness and agency.* With hindsight I realize I was confronting a taboo I never knew I had. That taboo is reflected in the content of the play I was trying to finish.

How I Got Here

It's 1995. I'm 45 years old. I am revisioning the Greek playwright Euripides' version of the ancient myth of Medea, the woman who infamously murdered her children. Please bear with me as we weave together some common threads between Medea, my mother and me. And, I believe, 'everywoman.'

First, the plot of Euripides' play: Medea falls in love with the Greek hero, Jason, who has travelled to her country to seize the prized treasure of her land ~ The Golden Fleece. This pelt of a magical, golden-woolled ram hangs on an oak tree, guarded by a never-sleeping Dragon. Whoever possesses it gains kingship authority and divine protection. But when Medea's father, the king, demands Jason accomplish impossible, death-dealing tasks to win the prize, Medea uses her sorceress powers to save Jason's life and enable his victory. She then sees her father plots to kill Jason anyway, so with a magical potion she puts the guardian Dragon to sleep, and together she and Jason escape with the magical Fleece to Greece. They marry. Medea produces two sons. Jason abandons her to marry a younger woman, Creusa, the daughter of the Greek king. This king fears Medea's vengeance so he exiles her, without her children. Before her exile Medea feigns forgiveness by delivering a wedding gift to Creusa, a cloak which burns her to death. In Euripides' classic version Medea completes her revenge on Jason by slaying their two young sons. In my version she slays them for a very different reason, which we shall soon see.

I became fascinated with Medea's story in the late 1970s. Before writing my version in 1995, I had covered a lot of ground and spiritual growth as a woman. I had gone from converting to Mormonism at age 19, to leaving the church at age 32, to then feeling suspended in spiritual limbo. Finally, in the mid-1980s, at age 35, I stepped onto the path of Goddess and feminist spirituality as both teacher and perennial student. What I learned on this spiritual path generated insights into Medea's plight that I have not seen presented anywhere else. I had awakened to the underlying misogyny ~ demonization, fear and suppression ~ of women's power, wisdom and self-sovereignty.

I am not the only one fascinated with Medea. Numerous productions continue to be mounted, however none bring through what I see in the myth. Context and root. Symptom and cause.

I see Medea as the epitome of Woman trapped in patriarchy.

Thus my title, "Medea Everywoman." I wanted Medea to tell her own story through which she gains these insights for herself, and for us, for Medea could not name patriarchy; she was born into it as we all are. How does a fish name water? It doesn't know there is anywhere else to live. *Naming* an obstacle gives us greater capacity to heal and liberate ourselves from it. The classic myth does not illuminate the underlying misogyny that drove Medea to her acts, and so does not afford a vision of healing. How can a myth about a woman who murders her children bring healing? We'll see how in "Medea Everywoman."

Though Medea tells her story to modern women, I maintain the mythic scope by placing it in a dreamscape.[1] Medea is conjured through the collective dream of three modern-day women, who represent women today, despairing for the condition of our world. A dreamscape touches our psyche at a deep, collective level. It was this subconscious level, both personal and collective, that had immobilized me.

The three Dreaming Women first meet Medea as she rages in anguish over the loss of her children. (Unlike the classical ending

---

[1] In 2017 I revised the script from a one-woman show to include a chorus of three women. However, the concepts and actual storytelling remain as they were in 1995.

where she flies off into the heavens in a glorious chariot.) They express their own grief and entrapment to Medea: "Our children are dying, our trees are burning, our waters are drying up! We can hardly see or breathe through the smoke." Against all logic the women feel that resolution can only come when Medea re-lives her life ~ *to discover the deepest motive of her deed* ~ which will heal and liberate all. This underlying motive for healing makes the play profoundly relevant to today's global issues and women's relationship to them.

FEMALE SOVEREIGNTY AND THE MISSING MOTHER

One of the first insights I had about Medea's story was the absence of her mother. We see this in fairy tales, too. The mother is usually absent, dead even, often replaced by a cruel stepmother. Think Cinderella and Snow White. The inherent female sovereignty of the Motherline is erased and replaced with a father-line. The only way to trace a patriarchal line is to control women's bodily sovereignty through our reproductive power. Patriarchy enforces this unnatural order through religions based on the lie of male-god birth, which erases the Great Mother Goddess. The veneration of a Great Mother was global and far pre-dates the last 6,000 – 10,000 years of male domination. The Greek pantheon eliminated the Great Mother by fragmenting her into a competitive gaggle of squabbling goddesses.

In my play, Medea uncovers suppressed female sovereignty as she recounts using her magic to save Jason's life and gain him the Golden Fleece. While Jason publicly battles for the prize, she catches her mother's onlooking eye:

> *My mother's eyes are strangely empty. They showed how much she had lost, how little she had to give me. It all belonged to the king. It had not always been that way. My mother gave me what could not be the king's.*

> *She passed to me, her daughter, the magical charms I used to make Jason victorious over my father and his plot to kill the man I loved.*

We can view the magic as women's mystical, spiritual powers which we still have but have largely forgotten due to centuries of coerced economic and emotional dependence on a husband.

> *But as Jason was victorious, my mother lost her daughter! Yet, she turned her eye from what I was about to do to her husband and king, and let me find what happiness I could. That happiness was Jason.*

Medea's mother passed on vestiges of women's former power, but was "missing" (ineffectual) to the extent that she could only aid Medea through her silence, for she herself was subject to the control of husband and king.

Medea uncovers another insight into repressed female power as she recalls putting the guardian Dragon to sleep so she and Jason can escape with the Fleece.

> *As a child I would sit for hours and gaze at the Dragon. One particular day, I only now recall, I awake in the pre-dawn to a warm flow between my legs, brightening my sheets with a red flame like the Dragon's fire. I feel compelled to go to the Dragon.*

When women dare to follow the pull of our life-giving blood, we experience the magnetic primal power of the Great Mother.

> *Even in the shrouded light Her iridescent scales glimmer. Her nostrils flare. She smells my blood. She lifts Her head to the first ray of sunlight. Fiery prisms of orange, vermillion and gold ignite down her back. She arches her great neck, turns her head and points Her*

eyes at me. Eyes that never close, eyes that always guard the Treasure of my father the king.

Eyes that speak to me. She is speaking to me! A language, forgotten, forbidden. Only once, this moment and never again is she speaking to me. Her golden eyes open visage to depths in her heart and there I see — infinite grief. She curves her neck about, peruses the cave behind her where the Golden Fleece hangs before it on the oak. In that moment I know — She is captive, guarding a Treasure that was once Her own.

I want to move past the oak with its golden, dead thing hanging on it. Past it, into the darkness of the cave behind. It pulls me. It pulses, full of life, like a heart, a womb.

But when I visited the Dragon with Jason, I poured my sleeping potion. I closed — our eyes. I see now, I knew, in that forbidden language, I knew then, while I leapt from the altar with the golden thing at one breast and Jason at the other, I leapt from one slavery to another. Yet, now I was a traitor to my homeland. Where could I go but forward?

OCEANIC FEELINGS

Remember me on the ocean floor, paralyzed by I didn't know what? Lying there, immobilized and desperate for a way to move forward, I finally realized the internal block: *If I perform this play it will kill my mother.*

What? If I perform this play it will kill my mother? It made no sense, especially since I had a good relationship with my mother. Yet this felt as literal to me as the floor I was flattened on. I had no rational explanation and maybe that's the whole point ~ I moved forward into my fear because, understanding or not, I felt compelled. Like Medea going to the Dragon.

Understanding came only after the act of power was completed. But here, I can give you some sense of the ocean metaphor my subconscious had presented. For that I credit feminist author Catherine Keller who in her brilliant book *From a Broken Web: Separation, Sexism and Self* gave me many insights that sparked my version of Medea's story, particularly her analysis of the classical "hero."[2]

Keller describes "oceanic feelings," the felt sense that we are not separate beings, but connected at a fundamental level to all that is. She contrasts women's relational attunement to this oceanic reality with the "hero" who tries to stave off his terror of oceanic feelings by holding rigidly to the illusion of a solid, unchanging self. He does this, ironically, through lots of action ~ roaming, rampaging, fighting, garnering "victories" as Jason did. He is an emotionally unavailable man. Nothing touches him, nothing moves him; if anything or anyone tries, he subdues and conquers them. We see the damage of such men in our modern world of war, rape, pollution, sex trafficking, you know the list.

Just what was my oceanic submersion trying to connect me with? Like Medea I live in patriarchy where the Great Mother is missing. Like Medea I have a mother who cared but who was missing to some degree. (Are not all mothers in patriarchy missing to some degree, and are not all daughters feeling this on some level?) I too gave my power away to men, as Medea did to Jason. As my mother did to my father.

---

[2] Many are familiar with "the hero's journey" eloquently described by Joseph Campbell and accoladed in legends and movies. But please consider the classic hero's actions in both Euripedes' version and mine: He steals the treasure of another country, betrays the woman who saves his life and enables his success, then abandons her for a younger woman and feels entitled to keep the children she bore him while she is exiled.

"Mom, why did you never talk back to Dad when he'd say you didn't know what you were talking about?"

"Well, honey, I wanted to keep the peace."

Mom and I occasionally had a shared experience that we never named. It was a particular quality of laughter when one of us, not knowing how funny it would strike us, casually mentioned something that Dad had done or said. Suddenly we were giggling like school girls, trying to repress our laughter, which only made it funnier and more forbiddenly delicious. Doubling over, laughing until tears sprang out of our eyes, we conspired in an unnamed bath of relief. We could never have explained what was so funny. It was about my father and her husband, but so much more. A spontaneous elixir for our smothered rage.

We also shared being tomboys ~ a young girl who behaves like a boy. A phase, it was said, that girls get over.

I would get over enjoying a body that was strong, vital, athletic, coordinated, tuned to exertion, sweat, muscle and strength? These qualities were so much a part of who I was I could not imagine myself without them. Tree climbing, swimming, catching crawdads in the creek, softball, volleyball, track and field. Tomboy!

Tomboy Mom had prided herself on having the best Tarzan call of all the kids. "Dad used to ask me to do the call for him," she said. I, too, sometimes got her to delight me with a nostalgic rendition. One particular day, when I was a teenager, I asked Mom to perform her Tarzan call for me. She hesitated but I enthusiastically prompted her.

"Come on, Mom, do it!"

"Ahhhh-ooh-aahh! ~ ooooh-aaah-aaah-aaah-aaaahhh!"

"Wow, Mom, that's great!" And it was. Then a sadness pushed its way up my chest toward my lips, but the words stopped at my throat, unformed. They would have been something like "What happened? Where did it go?" I didn't know what *it* was, except that it was too big, too deep to name. As deep as the grief in the Dragon's eyes. She had gotten over it.

I, too, got over it. When I was ten I proudly announced, —"I'm going to be the first woman President of the United States" but six years later I proudly announced: "My husband will never do the dishes!" Though my bid for president had a hint of female agency, I think it was based more on my male identification. Boys won at King of the Mountain (throwing others off a hill), were chosen first for dodge ball and became President of the United States. Boys mattered. I was not a sovereign girl, I was a tom-*boy*.

MEDEA'S EPIPHANY: THE DEEPEST MOTIVE OF HER DEED

We have seen Medea betray her homeland and herself, to benefit the hero she loved. We have seen her, in turn, betrayed by that same hero and husband, then stripped of home and children (exiled).

A pivotal point comes when Medea recounts murdering Jason's new bride, Creusa. Here, in my play, the murder of our ancestral mothers in the Burning Times overlaps with Medea's story and culminates in an unexpected epiphany. Medea becomes crazed as she describes Creusa bursting into flames when she dons the wedding cloak Medea gave her, Medea wheels about pointing and exclaiming, "She burns! She burns! There she burns! and there! and there! and there!" until she realizes:

> MEDEA: These — these — are not — Creusa. This is not my world.

> CHORUS: Another land. Another time!

> MEDEA: There — a woman big with child, roasting in flames. A cheering crowd cries "Burn her! The witch must burn!" Her belly bursts — macabre birth —— they toss the baby back to roast with the mother. Another pyre, another woman, her spirit rises above her flaming body but lingers long enough to see her daughter of five forced to dance upon the embers of her charred bones. A priest rubs the child's face with her mother's ashes so she does not forget. She does not forget.

Medea's vision continues with footbinding, rape, genital mutilation, until finally it culminates in the nuclear fire of Hiroshima. A stunned Medea states

> This is a vengeance beyond anything from my cauldron.

At the same time Medea somberly recognizes her complicity.

> Everywhere in your world I see the cold hunger of the hero I served into strength. I taste the bitter truth: There is no Jason without Medea.

In the chronology of the storytelling Medea now recalls the killing of her children. Exiled, she will be the missing mother, unable to protect her children, for what she birthed belongs to the father. She kills not out of vengeance, but because she knows her sons are doomed targets, obstacles to the inheritance of Jason's future sons.

> Better they die at the hands of she who loves them, than at the hands of those that hate them. This was

> how I slew my children, my flesh, my heart ~ quiet unrepenting mercy. It was the only way then. And now.

"Now" is the key to her deepest motive. In her vision she has seen the hero's endgame in the NOW of modern-day Women.

> It was the only way, then. And now.
> I now know the deepest motive of my deed.
> Hero, I will no longer love you into strength.
> I will no longer serve your wars
> to use that strength to kill.
> Nothing from me shall go forth into such a world.

As the Dreaming Women believed, this deepest motive heals and liberates. It serves life. They break the taboo of silence. They declare their sovereignty and wisdom. They name themselves:

> I am Woman. I am Mother. I am the Dragon protecting the Treasure. I am The Golden Treasure!

> MEDEA: At last I move past the greed that hoards a golden dead thing, death, hanging on a tree, worshipped. I move into the darkness of the cave, where the living Gold resides, in the loving, pulsing womb of Maa. Maa!

They invite the hero, self-severed from Life, to return from his illusory quests, to a world...

> ...Where Every man is a mothering son.
> Where Every woman is a mother of LIFE.
> Where Everywoman is Medea,
> rising in joy from the shrouds of grief,
> reborn.
> [End of play]

Life imitates art. Would I dare reclaim the Golden Treasure from male control? Or would I allow myself to remain captive as the Dragon? Would I dare break the silence? Move beyond smothered rage, keeping the peace, getting over it? Beyond the terrorist imprint of the Burning Times?

The dead weight of the ocean was beginning to stir. My oceanic immersion was an amniotic challenge to rebirth myself. What happens if I disobey the taboo of female sovereignty, if I liberate myself where my mother has not? Will I be betraying her? Negating her life? Will I cause her to feel her complicity in the ills of the world, and would that be too much for her to bear? But if I silence myself I will be consciously complicit, and can I bear that?

Naming complicity is not to condemn or blame, but by naming, liberate. I can't end the hero's rampage unless I own my complicity. This takes courage because for centuries women's very survival required complicity with male domination, to disobey could mean death. I believe all women feel this at some level.

OPENING NIGHT

I finished the script and crafted it as an actress, but my act of power was not complete. I had to actually perform the play to break the taboo. On opening night the oppressive ocean returned. I had so much back pain I was face down on the floor. Again, I literally could not stand up. Women friends gathered around me, massaged me, encouraged me, but the pain persisted. I rarely take even an aspirin but that night I took the pain pills offered to me. Drugged and able to stand, I took to the stage. The three scheduled performances were compelling enough that due to 'popular demand' we added a fourth.

In the following weeks several friends observed, "You look different! It's like a weight or a fog has been lifted off your forehead." More like an ocean, I thought to myself. In my journal:

"Dec 3, 1995. Medea Everywoman shifted so much in me…I no longer feel like a day job will suck the life out of me. I have more stamina, mental and therefore physical health."

Understanding emerges. What was my deepest motive in an act of power that I irrationally feared might kill my mother? It was to liberate myself from what my mother, and her mother before her, and her mother before her, could not. To know in my bones, the bones she gave me, that what frees me does not betray my mother, but honors and fulfills her mothering of me. My motive was to rise from oceanic paralysis into oceanic *feeling* ~ my desire and passion to rise sovereign, in joy, from the shrouds of our collective grief, reborn. I did it. And so can every woman.

ABOUT VAJRA MA

Rev. Vajra Ma teaches outside traditions and codifications, with warmth, humor and a bedrock compassion informed by her own dark nights of the soul. Since the late 80s she has guided women in our innate female bodywisdom through shamanic circles, voice work and the womb-sourced moving meditation she originated, The Dance of Feminine Power®. The author of *From a Hidden Stream: The Natural Spiritual Authority of Woman*, she is also published in eight anthologies including *Foremothers of the Women's Spirituality Movement*. Her award-winning website, Foremothers of Women's Spirituality and Their Living Wisdom for Today, includes 30 interviews with founders of the spiritual component of Second Wave feminism. With her late husband Wolfgang Nebmaier, she co-founded the non-profit Shakti Moon Foundation, dedicated to cultivating right relationship with Source, Earth and Woman as creatrix of future generations. Vajra Ma lives in the enchanted forests of southern Oregon with her dogs, cats, serpents and friendly wildlife. She holds ministerial credentials through the Temple of Diana, Inc.

"Women hold the keys to planetary peace. Let's unlock the doors together."

https://www.vajra-ma.com
https://www.facebook.com/vajra.ma/
www.womens-spirituality.org

Chapter 12

THE CAULDRON, A BAT AND BURNING DOWN THE HOUSE

Diana Will

IGNITING THE FIRE

Months ago, I felt an almost uncontrollable urge to burn it all. Everything. My journals, my writings, and even the beginnings of a novel about the sacred feminine. The feeling was so overwhelming that, in darker moments, I even thought of burning down my house. On alternating days, I found myself hiding under the covers, paralyzed by fear and anxiety. Out in the world, everything felt bleak: the relentless doom and gloom of bad news colored even sunny days with a grey haze of anger and frustration.

The 2024 Presidential election weighed heavily on my feminine soul. Inside, on a personal level, I worried incessantly about my family, especially my daughter and granddaughter as well as my older women friends. But at the core was my age. At 76, my faltering body's complaints grew louder, warning me of new aches, pains, and health challenges. Questions loomed: *Will my body hold up? Will I keep my mind? Will I have enough money to last another 10 or 15 years?* And perhaps most persistent of all: the age-old question: *What is wrong with me? Why am I still battling these demons at this age? What happened to the wise woman I thought I would become?* The weight of it all felt unbearable.

Worried about my declining mental health, I sought out Zoom therapy that I could do from bed. Having experienced therapy on and off during past challenges, I now demanded something more rigorous. "No gentle probing," I told my therapist. "Ask me the hard questions."

"Okay," he said, "Imagine you've poured the gasoline, lit the match and burned it all down. Your writings are gone. Your house is gone. Stand in the ashes. Did you save anything?" Closing my eyes, I imagined the scene. To my surprise, amid the ashes, I saw something untouched: my great-grandmother's mixing bowl, miraculously undamaged among the smoldering ashes. Then he asked me: "What comes next?" That last question stopped me in my tracks. I had been so caught up in my suffering, I had no post-destruction plan.

The vision of the bowl and hearing his question ignited a spark within me, not for destruction, but for transformation. Over the next few weeks, through therapy, my spiritual practice, soul searching conversations with close friends, reading, and reflecting, I slowly began to feel a shift. I climbed out of bed, put the matches away, and prepared for a new journey of rediscovery. I asked myself ~ How did I arrive here, at the doorstep of my 80s?

FILLING THE POT:
THE SYMBOLISM OF THE CAULDRON

When I was 70, I purchased my own home. It was a bold move, one that felt like reclaiming a piece of myself. In the backyard, I created a small sacred circle with a round fire pit at its center, edged in copper to resemble a cauldron. I had been researching the cauldron's symbolism for years. Cauldrons, bowls, pots and buckets have served humanity since ancient times for cooking, carrying, and storing. The cauldron can also be seen in a richer meaning as a container for emotional and spiritual transformation ~ where chaos brews and something new emerges. My circle and the stoked fire created a sacred space of possibilities, for nurturing self-empowerment and optimism for body, mind and soul. Not merely a symbolic relic of history; the cauldron can be a practical tool for navigating the tumult of our times and unleashing the collective intuitive power of the courageous feminine.

Here's why...

COLLECTING HERBS

Years before, while renovating a different house in Tucson, I had been working on a novel about the nature of the sacred feminine through history. One night I had an extraordinary encounter. I sat on my bed, writing about cauldrons and their role in women's history, especially during the witch trials and burnings. Suddenly, I noticed my bedroom door wiggle a bit. To my amazement and alarm, a bat flew in. It circled me as I ducked to the floor, covering my hair with my hands. I grabbed a blanket, attempting to wave it outside, but the bat lingered, spiraling around me before slipping through the door into the main part of the house. Following it cautiously, I saw the bat settle high on the brick fireplace wall. It wrapped its wings around its little body and disappeared into the shadows. I was fully awake. This was not a dream.

The next morning, standing in my living room, I excitedly shared what happened with my work crew. They howled and nearly fell over with laughter. They said, "You're a witch," and pointed fingers at me, turning their faces up to the sky with imagined fear. As we stood there, the bat suddenly returned, swooping down and circling us. Now swearing and yelling with true fright, they ran to their trucks and drove away like, well, bats out of hell. I was laughing in sheer delight. They did not return for 3 days until the foreman convinced them I was not actually a witch.

After they left, I heard a female voice that I did not recognize but instinctively knew was the bat. She told me to get a pencil and paper. She had a story to tell. Compelled, I did and wrote as fast as I could.

MEDICINE AND TINCTURES

She said:

> *"I was born in 1602 in Spain, the youngest of five sisters, and was known for my green eyes and long dark hair. My mother and grandmother were healers. They told me I was born with the gift. My grandmother was known as the 'death taker,' helping with the passage. We collected herbs, made medicines and tinctures, and earthlove to care for our village. In 1610, men came to our village demanding the women come out and give them access to our sacred knowledge.*
>
> *When we refused, women started running. In all the chaos, fear and running, they caught my hair, took me down and, with lifting and ripping, they raped me as my fingers dug into dirt. I did not cry. I was defiant. They mocked my fire. I spit at them, and one of them backhanded me. When they finished, they wanted healing for their leader, and they demanded our books. My grandmother was not there, so they turned to me. Grandmother had always told me that our book was 'The Precious,' the healing knowledge we learned through generations, and to keep it from harm. We knew its power. We also knew the stories of women being burned at the stake. Even with that fear of what might be coming, I would not give it up."*

The bat went on to tell me about how women wore grey and red dresses. She sewed red inside her cloak and embroidered red on the placket. In the evenings, they met in the forest and mountains where *The Great Mother* lived: Pound the thistle, scrape the bark, hold it to the sun for translucence and purity, select the right leaves ~ round, not pointed. This berry, not that one. Put them in the leather pouch or seal them in leaves for infusion. As she spoke, I could imagine them gathered around a large iron cauldron hung over a log fire. After she refused to give them the book, the men took her to a dungeon where she found her bruised grandmother. I could see it all. Finally, she said, "That's all for now. I will return some other day." But she did not. Since then, I learned that bat lore represents transformation, intuition, rebirth and courage.

STIRRING THE POT

After years of working, helping raise grandchildren, at the age of 72, I was ready to revisit the story and investigate its truth. To my shock, my research confirmed that from the 1500s until the 1800s, women accused of witchcraft were persecuted. 1610 was the year of witch trials in the Basque region of Spain. Her descriptions all aligned with historical accounts. I learned there was a Witch Museum for the 7000 examined, 41 accused and 7 burned at the stake.

Eager to understand what all this meant, I set off on a quest in 2022. Visiting the witch museum, Museo de las Brujas in Zugarramurdi, Spain, I was deeply struck by the room with hanging cauldrons ~ the spoons, stir sticks, ladles, drying herbs, and tincture jars ~ and by their bravery to continue healing practices in the face of possible death. Here, I felt no sense of time. It seemed the cauldron offered a mystical gateway ~ bridging my physical body with the spiritual realms. I was a 16th century healer. I was that young green-eyed girl. It was my hand on the wooden ladle stirring my pot. Their way of life, their bravery, felt familiar, real, and visceral.[3] I felt as though on a threshold. Seeing through a hundred eyes. Like holding both their stories and the medicine for all things, but not yet knowing the things.

---

[3] See https://en.wikipedia.org/wiki/Basque_witch_trials and https://courses.washington.edu/hsteu305/Henningsen%20Spain.pdf

Selecting the Leaves ~ Round, Not Pointed

Over time, I began to lead sacred circles as a way of creating healing opportunities for women. Under the light of the full moon, we drummed, laughed and danced. We shared our tears and triumphs while birthing new creations. We hugged, howled and released our fears and regrets into the flames, challenging our pain of outdated beliefs. The destructive and insulting "something is wrong with me" is tenacious, and its tentacles reach back thousands of years. We called upon our ancestors, goddesses, and angels, honoring the Great Mother in all her forms.

Using all our senses, we could inhabit our bodies, not just our minds. We shared meals, serving our handcrafted foods from beautiful dishes and inherited bowls. Around the table, alongside the cauldron fire pit, each could be safely seen and heard as we allowed our truths to flow freely. Each woman had a story that, at its core, felt familiar. Sharing knowledge and nurturing intuition, we underwent our own transformations. The circle and fire created a sacred space of joy, possibility, strength and optimism in our hearts, bodies, and souls. This became a conduit for unleashing the collective power of our courageous feminine.

Backhanded

Growing up in a multigenerational, deeply patriarchal Christian household, I learned early that women were to be silent and submissive. But that message went against my nature. Even with all the oppressive voices and rules to the contrary, my ancestral soul ~ the courageous wild feminine ~ longed for recognition, release and expression. I rebelled in small acts of defiance, even as I was increasingly muzzled.

As a young girl, I bristled under the concept I learned in Sunday school that I shared responsibility for all sin in this world due to

Eve's original sin. When I questioned these beliefs, I was labeled disruptive, and the male teacher reported my behavior to my father. He told me to be quiet and learn. Still, I tested my limits. I purposely rammed my bicycle into the back of our garage at full speed. My wildness dared me to walk heel-to-toe with my arms spread across picket fences. I slipped once and put a gash in my chin ~ still a scar of honor. On any swing set, I would swing as high as possible and jump off, one time breaking my arm. It was worth it. I was braver than a boy. Secretly, I would climb the highest tree on windy days and dream that I was flying, filled with hope of eventual escape. I look back now with gratitude and pride at the young me.

But things happened to me that started to quell this spirit. One summer when I was 11, the son of a neighbor molested me. He told me to be quiet and let him do what he wanted if I wanted to be his friend. I understood my body was not my own. When I was 12, I was informed by the shortest boy in middle school that I, the tallest girl, was the ugliest girl. Having no proof to the contrary, I accepted it. When I was 13, I rolled my eyes at something my mother said. My father leapt up, reached over the dinner table, and, with his full weight, punched me in the face, knocking me backward into the wall, unconscious. He taught me that physical punishment was needed to control my pre-teen female body.

By 14, I understood my role and expectations. Once, while yet again having to babysit yet my 7-year-old brother, I, in a rage, forced him over the edge of the dark cellar stairs with my mother's kitchen knife to his throat. I don't know what stopped me. In hindsight, years later, I realized that my little brother, dubbed "the little prince," whom I actually loved, was the physical stand-in for the abstract patriarchal boot on my neck.

By my late teens, I had little faith in myself, my abilities, or my future. The bubble had burst under the weight of misogyny.

And my mother remained caged still. I call these years the "Before Times."

SEALED IN LEAVES FOR INFUSION

In the 1960s and 70s, however, the Women's Liberation Movement changed everything. Icons like pioneers Betty Friedan and Gloria Steinem gave women like me permission to break free from societal constraints of the "Before Times." It was an exciting and heady time! I became a proud, card-carrying, movement-marching member of the early wave of baby boomers embodying the spirit of "Hear Me Roar."

The movement unleashed a wave of change that gave us choices our mothers never dreamed of. We could have careers, climb as high as we wanted ~ even aim for the presidency. Or, if we chose, we could stay home and focus on our families. For the first time, women could *decide* whether to have children or not and shape their lives on their own terms. I began to blossom! At 21, I took the brave step of ending the required marriage I had entered at 18 to get out of the house. I took my name back and paid my own way to college.

Younger women today, especially those under 60, often take these hard-won rights for granted. To them, the freedoms we fought for seem like an unchangeable part of life, just the way things are and will always be. However, we older women are keenly aware of the insidious persistence of misogyny (defined as prejudice and contempt against women and girls) and patriarchy (the system in which men as a group are constructed as superior to women as a group, and as such have authority over them). Today, in 2025, we see the old playbook back in use as women's choices are poised and planned to be rolled back.

Here are just a few of the rights we fought for:

1969 ~ California adopted the nation's first "no fault" divorce law, allowing divorce by mutual consent.
1972 ~ Title IX prohibited sex discrimination in all aspects of education programs that receive federal support. Women can play sports!
1972 ~ The U.S. Supreme Court ruled that the right to privacy grants not just married women, but also single women, the right to use contraceptives.
1973 ~ Roe v. Wade: the U.S. Supreme Court declared that the Constitution protects the right of women to terminate an early pregnancy, thus making abortion legal in the United States.
1974 ~ Women were able to get credit cards in their own names. Before, a man's signature was needed to apply for a credit card.

POUND THE THISTLE

One pivotal moment in my understanding of the generational nature of misogyny came when my daughter was 12. We traveled cross-country to my family home. I stepped out onto the back porch, where my father and a brother-in-law were seated around the now male-tended BBQ, watching her and her young cousins engage in a soccer game. I watched her fly across the green grass, her long blonde hair glistening as she outran her male cousins. My heart swelled with pride as my radiant young goddess, Athena, scored a goal, laughing and high-fiving everyone. She was a powerhouse, fully alive, and a natural competitor.

As they returned to the line of scrimmage, my father remarked, "You better sit on that girl." I froze, shocked. "What?" I responded quietly, feeling the weight of respect due to the male head of the family. It was 1992, and I was 43, still indoctrinated to accept men's words as gospel. "You heard me," he said. "You'll turn her into a lesbian," added the other font of wisdom, my brother-in-law. Now every fiber of my being wanted to yell, "Fuck you!" But instead, my face turned red, my throat dried up, and I quietly sputtered, "Never."

SCRAPE THE BARK

The realization struck hard: generational misogyny was being passed down to my daughter, and they expected me to enforce it. I bolted from the porch, ran onto the grass, and embraced my daughter and, in a moment of disobedience and rebellion, declared loudly, "You are amazing. I am so proud of you." Tears in my eyes, I looked back at those men, feeling the primal protective rage of a mother bear. I wanted to confront them, to rip off their heads and shove their words back down their throats. But I remained silent. Just like my mother.

THIS BERRY, NOT THAT ONE

As time moved on and I have grown older, wiser and stronger, I have learned that the image of women gathering around a cauldron, creating and befriending, shows up for me now as a fierce source of protection and inspiration. I can imagine all the powerful women throughout history protecting their children, their home, their lives. Today, my daughter, now 45, still has her remarkably wise, stand-alone spirit raising her boys. Her self-assuredness gives me hope for this generation of women.

And I know without a doubt: today I could chastise my father if he were still alive.

EARTHLOVE

Writing this story has been an act of awakening my instinctual power and wisdom. Wanting to burn down my house wasn't just a metaphor. It was a call from spirit, from my inner 'wild woman', a call for change, growth, and transformation. It also symbolizes, for me, the needed and coming burning or dismantling of structures suppressing women's voices and choices. I know some women are happy as they are and do not agree. I respect that. We each live our lives as we see fit. But even my mother, after years of struggling with her duty in keeping me down, whispered to me near her death, "Don't ever change." What a gift.

From standing in the ashes, I've made profound changes for my health and finances, embraced simplicity, and revealed deeper heart-centered clarity and resilience. I honor my intuition and the bubbling up again of my adventurous nature. My unleashed courage and sacred feminine have grown stronger, wiser, and ready for what lies ahead. And I finally ejected the shortest boy and other demons out of my head. Damn!

I'm reinvigorating my women's groups, focusing on late-life dreams and goals for myself, and inviting others to join me. I plan to travel to more sacred sites honoring women and write about it. I see and feel the ancestors, the courageous women before me, urging us to protect our progress and demand true equality. And, with hope, and needing much further conversation regarding this equality, I have amazingly been asked by a few men recently for inclusion in helping them reclaim their sacred masculine.

THE PRECIOUS

What I take from my life experiences is this. We, the older women ~ the crone goddesses, the wise elders ~ are needed now more than ever. As explorers, teachers, and revolutionaries, we've been shaped by triumphs and trials. We are the most educated, financially savvy, and longest-living generation in American history. The same wild brave spirit that propelled me and others during the Women's Liberation Movement now inspires us to demand true equality. Because today, many in power threaten the freedoms we've fought so hard to achieve. I, for one, will not let these rights slip away from my daughter, granddaughter, or today's young women. We each can do something, no matter how small. We can do hard things. We can bring joy and creativity. Our Mother Earth cries out for leadership that embodies compassion, collaboration, inclusion, flexibility, strength, and understanding ~ the timeless spirit and attributes of the feminine.

Together, gathering around the cauldron reminds us of our power to transform chaos into creation, to reclaim our stories, and to rewrite the narrative. Its flames call us to unleash the courageous feminine power already inherent in our souls, to stir the pot, and continue the work of co-creative and mystical transformation. And damn straight, if/when the revolution comes, I'm all in.

We've risen before. We will rise again.

P.S. A bat recently moved in under my eaves...

About Diana Will

From the earliest days of the Women's movement in the 60's, Diana has been an enthusiastic way-finder of creativity, adventure, dreams and playing life full out. For 40 years, with a BS in Social Work, she created and administered unique programs for her clients, ranging from abused children to seniors with dementia.

Since retirement, she has become an EponaQuest Instructor, a Reiki Master and a HeartMath Coach. Spiritually, she practices Nichiren Buddhism as a women's leader, and conducts goddess gatherings around a sacred circle at her home in Tucson, AZ. She is grateful to be a mother, grandmother and wise elder.

Free gift: One lesson in Heart Breathing ~ Feel uplifted and alive, less rushed, more peaceful. Deepen connections to those you love.

Email: **TravelWithSkygoddess@gmail.com**
Instagram:
https://www.instagram.com/goddessmyoho/?hl=en
Website: **https://myteacher.horse/**

Epilogue

How I Healed from Incest to Awaken to the Divine Feminine Within

Laura Joan Cornell, PhD

This is my #MeToo story. It's also the story of how I recovered my connection to myself, to my mom, my dad, and to the Divine Feminine.

Like all #MeToo stories, this story is not fun to tell. It's gut wrenching to spell out how bad everything was in my worst moments, as I would prefer to live in the beautiful present, and in gratitude. I am grateful for the present ~ my sweet husband, friends and community that surround me, fulfilling work, tender connections with all my family members, a lively connection with my inner life and with Spirit, Source. I have come to be grateful for my past as well and I realize that my life is blessed.

But I tell this story here as a form of service, for others who may have experienced something similar, and also for myself, as a way of continuing to sew together the pieces of my life.

Experiencing incest broke me apart. Like a frozen river whose deep waters continue to move freely, but whose surface cracks and breaks into jagged chunks, I was unable to deal with the natural flow of my emotions or to face the challenges of adolescence and young adulthood in a healthy way. I turned instead to broken, jagged coping behaviors.

The year is 1978. I am 15 years old and have my first period. I am so embarrassed by my body and its bleeding that I hide my bloody underwear in a drawer. I am so disconnected from my mother that it never occurs to me to tell her, or to ask her to buy me menstrual pads. Somehow she finds the underwear in the drawer and looks at me in surprise. "Why didn't you tell me?" she asks. I am utterly ashamed.

In my freshman and sophomore years of high school I am lonely, isolated, and afraid to go into the lunchroom. I sometimes eat my lunch hiding in the bathroom. While I develop close friendships in my junior and senior years, the inner experience of isolation continues.

After high school, I go through several painful years of binge eating, extending into my early 20s. I eat a normal meal, then one dessert, then another, then some more bread, and then another dessert. I hear a distant voice inside my head saying "This is awful. You should stop," but I feel compelled to continue.

Sometimes, I secretly stuff down as many crackers, cookies, chips, and peanut butter as I can find. I am terrified someone will walk in and see me. After one of these episodes, I try to vomit the food up, as I feel sick to my stomach. Fortunately, I'm not able to make myself throw up, or I'm convinced I would have become bulimic.

The final straw is when I come down with pneumonia and then immune fatigue. Just four years after college I get a type of pneumonia that only the elderly or hospitalized usually get. Two rounds of antibiotics later I am still sick. After 6 weeks, I go back to work as an elementary school teacher, much weakened.

The stress of multiple years of unhealthy eating and little exercise, combined with not having any means to soothe my frayed nervous system, catches up with me. Over the next several years I find myself chronically ill, either having a cold or flu, just getting over one, or about to get one. I see no way out of this state and come to accept it as normal.

My life might have continued this way if not for the grace of an accident at work. I fell and was sent to a chiropractor, who treated not only my back, but diagnosed me with immune fatigue and told me to go to yoga. This was a major turning point that would change the course of my life.

I still remember my first yoga class in 1992. My body was unfamiliar with the poses and many of them felt uncomfortable. But most of all I remember the teacher saying not to compare ourselves with anyone else in the room, but instead to go at our own pace. This self-acceptance was a radical concept for me.

My energy level improved immediately, and I was able to go out dancing the next evening after work, something I hadn't done in years. I quickly became a dedicated yoga practitioner, and a certified instructor 3 years later.

Yoga not only gave me the means to heal my immune and nervous systems, but helped me to go deeper still. Through yoga I learned to gently access my emotions and explore them within, creating a safe container for integrating painful childhood memories. I would return to this container repeatedly for the next several decades, coming home to myself and over and over again as I untangled the web of my past.

I came to understand what was behind the binge eating, and was able to release it. I realized that being physically heavy provided some twisted form of safety and security for me. Guys wouldn't notice me, and I didn't have to compete for attention or being liked. I could just be a nobody. As I came to feel safer in my body this became less necessary.

I also realized that by overeating I unconsciously tried to companion my mom, who was constantly going on and off of diets, not happy with her weight. On the one hand, Mom was a beautiful woman who carried herself well. She was a plus-size model for Dillards, participating in fashion shows in exchange for shopping gift cards. On the other hand was her repeated dieting.

A therapist helped me see through this. "Don't you think that if you want to companion your mom, she would rather have you happy and healthy?" This was a great insight, and I realized that being my best self ~ not holding myself back ~ was the way to be her friend in life.

As much as yoga was helping me to ground my emotions, I longed for more ways to connect with other women and with my own feminine being. I learned a sequence of yoga poses called the Moon Salutation, which was created to balance and strengthen a woman's body. Fascinatingly, this yoga flow was specifically designed to support the unique phases of a woman's life cycle ~ menstruation, pregnancy, and menopause. For me, doing these poses helped heal the shame and disconnection I had experienced as a teenager about my menstrual flow.

The Moon Salutation was also created to honor feminine values of relationship, openness, and connecting with the earth. The Moon Salutation brings women together in sacred circle, something I dearly love. I decided to write my Masters Thesis on this yoga flow, exploring it through interviews with senior yoga teachers as well as through in-depth reading on women's psychology.

As part of this research on women's psychology, I studied books on sexual trauma, women's disconnection from our bodies, and incest, all of which I had experienced. While I had discussed the incest in therapy earlier, I came to understand even more clearly how it had affected me, and how important it was to address it directly.

I read that in father-daughter incest, the daughter is cut off from her mother and thus her own inner feminine. This made complete sense to me. I committed to heal my relationship to myself, my mom, and my own inner Divine Feminine. One step in that healing was telling the truth about the trauma I had experienced as a child.

When I was a toddler my dad had trouble controlling his temper. My sister and I were spanked on multiple occasions, although I have almost no memory of these incidents. I did, however, hear my mom repeatedly tell the story of my dad "losing it" on me when I was a toddler. Mom said she had to pull me away from him and that I was black and blue the next day.

For many years she would tell this story as a joke, as if to laugh at what a strange husband she had. Finally in my late 30s I asked her if that story were true, and she said that yes, it was. I responded, "That's not funny Mom, that's really sad." Mom replied, "I'm sorry. You're right, it's not funny." I never heard her speak of the incident again.

My mom loved her husband dearly, and very much wanted to create a good life with him. But things weren't easy, and raising children is complex. Neither of my parents was well equipped to help my sister and me manage our emotions, love our bodies or learn about sex with grace.

When I was 7 my father decided to "educate" me about the male body, exposing himself to me without telling my mom, and asking if I'd like to touch. Something so out of context with the rest of my life and so unknown to my mom was completely terrifying to me. The only dream I remember from childhood was of my father chasing me with a knife on a burning ship.

When I was a pre-adolescent, it was my dad, not my mom, who talked with me about expecting my period, telling me that he tracked my mom's cycle on his calendar, and that he would be happy to do the same for me. And it was my dad, not my mom, who talked with me about sex and their couple relationship. These conversations humiliated and traumatized me.

My emotions were frozen from these experiences, and I felt existentially lonely from my mom's absence in my life emotionally. Therapy helped me to understand that I needed to tell my mom what had happened. Thankfully, when I told her she believed me, and supported my moving forward in the way that felt right to me.

Discussing the incest wasn't easy for me, and it was several years before I was ready to talk to my dad about it. I first wrote him a letter, and awaited his reply. I felt sick to my stomach when I got an envelope in the mail from him, knowing it held his response.

This began a bumpy process of communication. My mom insisted that my dad listen to me and enter into dialogue. We went through a day of family therapy, and at the end he said he understood why his actions were inappropriate. It would be more than a decade later before he was able to express his emotions about all of this, saying he felt "terrible" when he realized he had harmed me.

While things were still bumpy between us for a while, I felt freedom in no longer having a secret to hide. I was grateful to my parents for having extended way beyond their comfort zone to hear me. And I felt empowered in knowing that speaking my truth could have a positive impact on our family.

So many others factors in my life conspired to support me. When I look back, I have a sense of the Divine Mother walking along beside me, pulling me forward toward wholeness.

Despite tremendous inner brokenness, I had a deep desire to connect with others. As a junior in college, I noticed that all of my friends except me were dating, and I decided to do something to change that. I went to the health center and spoke with a therapist, then signed up for a non-credit but comprehensive course on human sexuality. Two months later I found myself head-over-heels in love with a smart, gentle man. We were a perfect match ~ neither of us had ever kissed anyone before ~ and the next two years of puppy love and budding sexuality were incredibly healing.

Other positive factors included my connection with nature, in which I found great peace walking in cornfields, forests, the mountains or by the ocean. My love of movement as a child led to the pleasure I found in dance, which took full bloom later when I learned yoga. Many years of worshiping with Quakers, circling with women, and practicing meditation all helped me come home to the light within, which continues to guide my life to this day.

In 2011 I founded Divine Feminine Yoga to highlight women's healing and empowerment through yoga. To me, Divine Feminine Yoga means embodied wholeness. It's a way of helping ourselves recover from the cultural wound of disconnection from the feminine, the core injury we all experience in patriarchy, no matter the personal details. It's calling ourselves home to befriend our bodies and our inner wisdom. It's locating ourselves as daughters of the Divine Mother, and as such knowing that we are loved and cherished.

I soon became a business coach, supporting other women to strengthen their voice and achieve their purpose in the world. This work has been deeply fulfilling and I love it dearly. Years later, I would move into author coaching as well, helping women find their voice and tell their stories ~ such as in this book.

As I grew in my profession, I continued to understand and repair other ways I had been separated from my mom. And as I was growing and wanting to be closer to her, she was growing too. She learned to set boundaries with my dad and to enjoy the company of her children. She loved being a grandma, and commented that when she was younger she had forgotten to enjoy being a mom. I appreciated this insight on her part.

I loved watching the evolution of both of my parents as they grew older. They came to have a beautiful relationship, genuinely enjoying each other's company. They were honest and direct in dealing with conflict, and my dad humble and accepting of my mom's requests, which she was now able to make.

By the time she passed on, my mom and I enjoyed a close relationship. Whereas previously I had rejected her good qualities, I came to admire her deeply, and to want to be more and more like the best of her.

Some of my most tender times with Mom were just after illness or injury, when she would let me care for her gently, just as she must have done for me when I was an infant.

Once when I visited her after a cancer surgery, she joked to the nurses in the hospital that I was going to make her do yoga, and she was right, we did gentle yoga together, right there on her hospital bed. We read her Christian Science Lesson together when I would visit. I just wanted to read whatever my mom was reading, and to accompany her in that.

In her last few years, Mom couldn't reach to touch her feet, and would ask me to put lotion on her dried and cracked toes. I was happy to do this, and to have a way to express my love for her. I soaked her feet in warm salt water, using a brush or pumice stone to remove the dried skin, then would give her a foot massage with olive oil. She loved it.

I learned from studying Family & Systemic Constellations how important it is to honor both our mother and father. Life comes through them, and what a gift it is! After becoming a Constellations Facilitator 2 years ago, I decided to make a concerted effort to connect even more deeply with my dad.

Last summer I was able to visit my father and his new wife for a week at their lakeside cabin in Idaho. I carried with me a strong intention to tell my dad how much I love him. I asked for special time with him, and he agreed to pick me up at the airport and drive me the 2 hours to the lake. I brought with me my violin, which I'm playing again now after a hiatus of 50 years. Enjoying the violin with my dad on piano was a shared joy. I was able to look him in the eyes and specifically thank him for all the violin lessons he and my mom had shuttled me to, something I had never done. I played cards with Dad and Ginni, and we enjoyed little walks by the lake.

On the third day of my visit, something remarkable happened. My father fell into the lake, fully clothed, between their pontoon boat and the dock. The situation was perilous, as the afternoon winds were strong and the boat was lurching strongly in what was turning out to be a botched dock landing. My dad was sputtering and coughing, gasping for air in the water, and although he's normally a good swimmer, he was caught off guard, completely disoriented from the surprise of the fall and the heaviness of his long-sleeved, button-down shirt, pants, and leather shoes.

I realized how easy it would be for him to be battered between the dock and the lurching pontoons. I jumped into action and held the boat away from the dock using one leg. I reached down to grab my dad and guide him to safety. Once away from the pontoons, I cradled his head in one hand, holding him above the waves so he could breathe. I yelled for Ginni to throw me a life vest which I wrapped around his head. When we got him to shore he was still coughing up water, and needed me to help him stand. He leaned on me with all his weight. I realized how close we had come to losing him.

If I had not been present that day the outcome might have been very different. I believe that God or Goddess perfectly orchestrated this event to match my intention of expressing my love to my father by saving his life.

It takes courage to speak about what has harmed us. It takes courage to engage in dialogue. It takes courage to see the good and to love others even when they have caused injury. Every traumatic situation is different, and in mine, I have been able to stay in grateful and loving contact with both my parents.

Now when I think back on the incidents of harm, I see myself as a beautiful little girl. I hold this little girl and offer comfort, telling her how much I love her, and that she didn't do anything wrong. When I envision my father in those moments, I see him also as a little boy, and I see the suffering he incurred in his childhood. I feel compassion for both of us.

The growth and transformation I've had through these experiences are profound.

Every day I'm grateful that I can eat a normal meal and then stop. I now honor my body and respect its guidance. I feel the cycles of nature and the Divine Feminine moving through me.

I am grateful for profound and intimate connections with my husband and other family members. Most importantly, I know my life as sacred.

May all daughters be well supported on their journey, as I have been!

About Laura Joan Cornell, PhD

Laura Joan Cornell, PhD (Yogeshwari) is a best-selling author, and a sacred business and sacred writing mentor. She is founder of Divine Feminine Yoga, through which she has directed nine online conferences empowering women's voices, and where she offers coaching, retreats, online courses and leadership training for women worldwide.

Laura is author of the book *Moon Salutations: Women's Journey Through Yoga to Healing, Power, and Peace*. In previous work as Founder of the Green Yoga Association, Laura spurred a national movement towards Green Yoga studios, produced two major conferences on yoga and ecology, and sold 10,000 non-toxic yoga mats from her living room. She has been featured in Yoga Journal, Yogi Times, LA Yoga, and Common Ground magazines.

Laura lives with her husband and goldendoodle in beautiful Sedona, Arizona, where she enjoys hiking, gardening, and pickleball. This is her second anthology of sacred feminine stories.

www.DivineFeminineYoga.com
www.MoonSalutations.com

Acknowledgements

I want to express my sincere gratitude to all the teachers who guided me in excavating and trusting my stories. I'm especially grateful to Caroline Foster at the California Institute of Integral Studies (CIIS), my first writing instructor there. The "Organic Inquiry" research method I studied at CIIS profoundly shaped my thinking, teaching me the power of interviews and the transformative potential of personal narratives. Thank you to Tom Bird for illuminating the power of immersive writing and the importance of finding flow.

A special thank you to Audrey Silverman Foote, who supported me through years of somatic healing and preparation for my first brave venture into the publishing world, including the initial version of the chapter that appears here as the epilogue.

My deepest appreciation goes to the incredible team at Spotlight Publishing House. To Becky Norwood, thank you for your skillful management of the layout, cover design, publishing final details, and the countless other elements involved in marketing and promoting a new book. Your grace and professionalism were evident in every interaction with myself and the co-authors.

I am immensely grateful to Hyla Hitchcox, who served as our proofreader, copy editor, and chief cheerleader. Your friendly encouragement and insightful suggestions consistently improved the clarity of our writing. You made the entire process so much more enjoyable.

To Wendy Willtrout, thank you again for your tireless efforts as the "herder-of-the-cats," expertly gathering author photos and chapter versions, ensuring all materials reached Becky, and patiently answering countless questions from the authors. This project wouldn't have been possible without you!

My heartfelt thanks to my husband, who read every word of my chapter ~ multiple times ~ and listened patiently to my dreams and reflections as I explored the meaning of this project and my contribution to it. Your unwavering encouragement, during this and every writing journey, along with the love and support you and Millie provide, create the nurturing home and writing environment that make all of this possible.

To the authors, thank you for sharing so generously of yourselves. Your vulnerability, strength, and courage in telling these stories has been a profound gift to our Sacred Author Incubator. I know that each of you has grown not only through telling your own story but also through sharing this journey in community and being supported by one another. Your stories will benefit many women widely and be a great healing force far beyond our circle. My prayer is for you to receive all the blessings you desire from this generous act of courage.

Finally, I offer my deepest gratitude to Great Mother Spirit, the loving, wise presence I feel in every breath and daily meditation. I experience your physical presence in this beautiful earth, with which I am privileged to commune daily amidst the red rocks of Sedona. You hold and carry me always.

About the Cover Artist

Aimee Tomczak, MA, LMFT, is an Artist, Psychotherapist, Intentional Creativity Coach and Painting Instructor. Her colorful & soulful paintings begin with an intention and layered process inviting mystical guidance to reveal faces of the feminine and rhythms of nature through color and pattern.

Her cover art painting, "Spiral Woman," reveals a wise feminine presence unleashing her power through the spiral path of courage and transformation. This painting symbolizes each author's awakening into her full divine power by sharing her courageous story.

Aimee leads popular "Art as Medicine" workshops both online and in-person at Fulton Crossing Gallery in California. She is passionate about guiding people to rediscover and claim their joy, power and inner knowing through creative expression.

Aimee Tomczak

Get Aimee's free gift, "Claim Your Creative Space," a 10-minute guided meditation here:
https://mailchi.mp/7b5c0f82c0c9/ylgfnz1ybp

Learn about Aimee's online workshops and in-person offerings at **www.aimeetomczak.com**

View her Artwork, including originals, prints, and merchandise at: **www.aimeetomczakart.com**

Contact Aimee at: **Beloved3me3@gmail.com**

About Divine Feminine Yoga and Ananda Press

Divine Feminine Yoga was founded to help women heal ~ body, mind, and soul ~ so we can reach out to heal the planet.

Ananda Press features voices of wisdom in conscious conversation. Learn from soulful women who celebrate the Divine Feminine and Her transforming presence in today's world.

We offer:

- Global online conferences to inspire, uplift, and connect you with other lightworkers.
- Sacred writing immersions and courses, retreats, and mentoring.
- Sacred business courses, sister-mind support groups, and coaching.
- The opportunity to be featured in our books and online conferences.

Please join us to connect with like-minded women and expand and empower your voice.

Learn more and stay in touch:

DivineFeminineYoga.com
100 Sedona Street
Sedona, AZ 86351
888-423-8843

ALSO BY LAURA JOAN CORNELL, PHD

MOON SALUTATIONS:

WOMEN'S JOURNEY THROUGH YOGA TO HEALING, POWER AND PEACE

"Revelatory, insightful, fascinating, and beautiful. A must read for those women who practice yoga as well as those who don't."
—*Judith Hanson Lasater, PhD,* Author of Restore and Rebalance

"Laura has given us a great gift through the birthing of Moon Salutations!"
—*Nischala Joy Devi,* Author of The Secret Power of Yoga

"A wise, full moon of a book."
—*Amy Weintraub,* Author of Yoga for Depression

Available on Amazon and through Ingram Spark.

Claim your free Moon Salutations mini-course:
www.MoonSalutations.com

The Flow Formula

Write Your Book with Ease

Get Unstuck, Find Your Rhythm, and Finally Finish Your Book.

You have a book inside you ~ waiting to be written. But if you've ever struggled with **writer's block, self-doubt, or overwhelm**, you're not alone.

The Flow Formula offers a **proven, intuitive method** to help you **tap into your creativity, trust your voice, and bring your book to life** ~ without the stress.

Inside, you'll discover:

- **3 simple steps to move from stuck to flow** ~ so you stop overthinking and start writing with confidence.

- **The 5 biggest mistakes that hold writers back** ~ and how to avoid them.

- **How to structure your book naturally** ~ so even complex ideas come together with ease.

- **The #1 myth that keeps new authors stuck** ~ and the shift that will finally help you finish your book this year!

Your book is ready. **Are you?**

Download your free guide now:
TheFlowFormula.How

www.ingramcontent.com/pod-product-compliance
Lightning Source LLC
Chambersburg PA
CBHW072156070526
44585CB00015B/1167